10 Steps to Effective Risk Management:

Turn Turmoil into Triumph

SANJAY THIYAGARAJAN

Copyright © 2024 Sanjay Thiyagarajan

All rights reserved. No part of this book may be reproduced, stored in a retrieval system, or transmitted in any form or by any means—electronic, mechanical, photocopy, recording, scanning, or otherwise—without the prior written permission of the publisher, except for brief quotations in critical reviews or articles.

This workbook is intended for personal use only and is not to be resold or distributed without permission from the author.

DEDICATION

To those whose sublime wisdom and exquisite grace have adorned my path, this study is dedicated with unfeigned reverence and esteem.

CONTENTS

INTRODUCTION	2
THE EVOLVING LANDSCAPE OF WORK	4
The Shift to Hybrid Work	4
What is Risk Management?	5
Why Agile Risk Management?	5
Chapter 1	10
UNDERSTANDING RISK MANAGEMENT	10
The Essence of Risk Management	12
Risk Identification:	13
Risk Assessment:	15
Risk Mitigation:	16
Risk Monitoring:	18
Agile Risk Management:	20
Chapter 2	23
THE DAILY LIFE OF A RISK MANAGER	23
Challenges in a Hybrid Work Setting	25
Functional Key Responsibilities:	25
Most common Challenges of a Risk Manager:	31
Navigating the Daily Life of a Risk Manager in a Hybrid Setting	35
The Importance of Your Role	36
Chapter 3	37
GLOBAL STAKEHOLDER MANAGEMENT	37
Effective Communication Techniques	39
Strategies for Managing Global Stakeholders:	40
Chapter 4	51
FRAMEWORKS AND PROCESSES	51
Exploring Risk Management Frameworks	53
COSO (Committee of Sponsoring Organizations) ERM Framework:	54

ISO 31000	58
NIST Risk Management Framework:	61
FAIR Model:	65
Agile Risk Management Framework:	68

Chapter 5 — 71
RISK MANAGEMENT CASE STUDIES — 71
Why are risk management case studies important? — 73

Chapter 6: — 85
RISK MANAGEMENT IN ACTION — 85
- Handling Real-Time Crises — 87

Chapter 7 — 99
TECHNOLOGY AND TOOLS — 99
- Leveraging Technology in Risk Management — 101

Chapter 8 — 110
BUILDING A RISK-AWARE CULTURE — 110
- Training Programs: Empowering Employees with Knowledge — 111
- Leadership Commitment: Setting the Tone from the Top — 112
- Open Communication: Encouraging Transparency and Reporting — 114
- Continuous Improvement: Adapting and Evolving — 115
- Real-World Applications and Outcomes — 116

Chapter 9 — 124
ADAPTING TO FUTURE UNCERTAINTIES — 124
- Increased Reliance on Technology: — 126
- How Big Data and Analytics Work in Risk Management? — 130
- Cybersecurity Technologies — 134
- Enhanced Regulatory Requirements — 138
- Focus on Resilience — 139

Chapter 10 — 143
EMBRACING A PROACTIVE RISK MANAGEMENT CULTURE — 143
APPENDICES — 149

ACKNOWLEDGMENTS

It is with the most profound and inexpressible gratitude that I extend my deepest appreciation to those who have played an indispensable role in the realization of this work. To my dearest parents, whose unwavering fortitude, boundless encouragement, and unswerving faith in my abilities have been my compass, I am eternally beholden. Their affection and support, an ever-present balm amidst life's vicissitudes, have been nothing short of a blessing beyond measure.

To my esteemed and venerable colleagues, whose perspicacity and sagacious counsel have enriched this intellectual pursuit, I offer my sincere thanks. Your unparalleled erudition and collaborative spirit have made this endeavor not only possible but immeasurably rewarding. It has been a rare privilege to walk alongside such exemplary minds, and for your indispensable contributions, I am deeply indebted.

To my most cherished and steadfast friend, whose constancy, loyalty, and unerring companionship have been a source of both solace and inspiration, I extend my heartfelt thanks. Your unwavering support has been a beacon in times of uncertainty, and for that, I am forever grateful.

To you, the discerning reader, I am profoundly indebted. Your engagement with these humble pages elevates them beyond the mere written word, imbuing them with significance and purpose. May this work, in all its intricacies and insights, serve as a worthy companion in your intellectual journey. It is for you, most esteemed reader, that these words have been meticulously crafted.

To each of you, whose influence and presence are felt in every syllable of this manuscript, I remain ever in your debt, and for that, I extend my most profound and everlasting thanks.

INTRODUCTION

"The secret of change is to focus all your energy not on fighting the old, but on building the new."

— Socrates

THE EVOLVING LANDSCAPE OF WORK

The world of work has undergone a tectonic shift, a transformation stimulated by the global pandemic that forced millions to rethink how, where, and why we work. Suddenly, the daily commute became a thing of the past, office corridors fell silent, and dining tables turned into workstations. As organizations scrambled to fit into this abrupt change, they stumbled upon a new way of working—one that blends the convenience of remote work with the collaborative energy of in-person interactions. Welcome to the new normal.

The Shift to Hybrid Work

Hybrid work environments, where employees split their time between home and the office, have become increasingly common, especially since the global pandemic. Many companies had to quickly adapt to remote work to ensure the safety of their employees. As the situation evolved, a blend of remote and in-office work emerged, offering both flexibility and new challenges.

Initially, the transition to remote work felt like a temporary solution, a quick fix to keep the wheels going during an unprecedented global crisis. But as weeks turned into months, and months into years, it became evident that remote work wasn't just a passing phase. Organizations began to see the benefits of this model: increased flexibility, access to a broader talent pool, and often, heightened productivity. Employees, too, found value in the flexibility, relishing the newfound work-life balance as an addon of remote work.

However, the hybrid model is not without its challenges. Balancing remote and in-office work requires a careful orchestration of resources, a rethinking of workplace culture, and, crucially, a robust approach to risk management. This is where agile risk management comes into play, offering a framework that emphasizes adaptability, responsiveness, and resilience.

What is Risk Management?

Risk management might sound complex, but it's essentially about being prepared for uncertainties that could impact an organization's operations. Think of it as a safety net. If you're crossing a busy street, risk management would be looking both ways before you cross, so you avoid getting hit by a car. In a business context, it involves identifying potential problems (risks), assessing their likelihood and impact, and then figuring out how to prevent or handle them.

Why Agile Risk Management?

Agile risk management is like being a skilled surfer. You need to be flexible and responsive to the waves (challenges) that come your way. Traditional methods might be too rigid and slow, but agile approaches allow organizations to quickly adapt to changes, making them more resilient. This is especially important in a hybrid work environment where situations can change rapidly.

In a hybrid work environment, risks can emerge from various fronts i.e. cybersecurity threats, communication breakdowns, and operational disruptions, to name a few. Traditional risk management approaches, often characterized by rigid procedures and slow response times, are inappropriate to address the dynamic nature of these risks. Agile risk management, however, embraces change, encourages continuous feedback, and fosters a culture of proactive risk identification and mitigation.

Imagine a typical day in a hybrid work setting. You start your morning with a virtual team meeting, discussing the priorities for the day and any potential risks on the horizon. As you sip your coffee, you receive an alert about a new cybersecurity threat targeting your industry. Thanks to the agile risk management framework your organization has adopted, you're not thrown into a panic. Instead, you activate a predefined response plan, quickly mobilizing your team to address the threat. By midday, the risk is contained, and you can shift your focus back to strategic planning, confident that your agile approach has shielded the organization from what could have been a major disruption.

This book aims to help you understand how agile risk

management can be your guiding light in the unpredictable world of hybrid work environments. Whether you're a seasoned professional looking to refine your skills or just starting, the principles and examples within these pages will provide practical insights and tools to manage risks efficiently. We will delve into the core principles of risk management, explore real-world case studies from leading companies, and provide you with the tools and techniques needed to navigate the uncertainties of the modern workplace.

Structure of the Book

We'll start with the basics of risk management and gradually dive deeper into specific frameworks and strategies used by successful companies. You'll learn about the daily life of a risk manager, how to handle real-time crises, and the importance of building a risk-aware culture. Each chapter will offer real-world examples and case studies to make the concepts clear and relatable.

One of the most compelling aspects of agile risk management is its focus on continuous improvement. In a hybrid work setting, conditions can change rapidly, and the ability to adapt quickly is paramount. Agile risk management promotes a mindset of ongoing learning and adaptation, encouraging teams to regularly review their processes, learn from past experiences, and iterate on their strategies. This iterative approach not only enhances your ability to manage risks but also drives innovation and resilience within your organization.

Throughout the book, we'll share stories from various industries, such as finance and technology. These examples will show how different companies have successfully managed risks in hybrid work settings. By the end of this book, you'll not only understand the theory but also see how it applies in real-world scenarios.

In the chapters that follow, we will also explore the critical role of technology in risk management. From AI and machine learning to data analytics and cybersecurity tools, technology offers powerful solutions to the challenges posed by hybrid work environments. We'll look at how these tools can be leveraged to enhance risk identification, assessment, and mitigation, enabling you to stay ahead of the emerging threats.

Furthermore, we'll explore the human side of risk management. It's not just about implementing processes and technology; it's about engaging people. Establishing a mindset that prioritizes risk within your organization is key to successful risk management. We'll share strategies for promoting open communication, encouraging proactive risk reporting, and making sure everyone understands their role in managing risks.

Finally, we'll bring everything together with a discussion on future trends and the evolving landscape of risk management. As we look ahead, one thing is clear: the only constant is change. By embracing the principles of agile risk management, you can help your organization navigate the uncertainties of the future with confidence and resilience.

As we embark on this journey together, I invite you to keep an open mind, embrace change, and be ready to adapt. The hybrid work environment is here to stay, and with the right approach to risk management, you can turn potential challenges into opportunities for growth and innovation.

Let's get started.

Chapter 1

MAPPING THE RISK LANDSCAPE

"The only real mistake is the one from which we learn nothing." — *Henry Ford*

Welcome to the first chapter of our exploration into risk management. Here, we will delve into the basics, unpacking the core principles, processes, and methodologies that form the foundation of effective risk management. Get comfortable, maybe with a cup of coffee in hand, and let's begin this enlightening journey together.

The Essence of Risk Management

Risk management isn't just about defense; it's about taking proactive steps too. Think of it as managing a large event like a wedding. It's not just about reacting to things that go wrong, but about planning ahead to ensure everything goes smoothly. At its core, risk management involves anticipating unexpected issues, preparing for unforeseen events, and minimizing their impact on an organization's goals.

Consider yourself as the wedding planner for a major event. Before the big day, you meticulously plan every detail, taking into account potential problems such as bad weather, vendor cancellations, or last-minute changes to the guest list. You ensure that there are contingency plans in place, like indoor venues in case of rain, backup vendors on standby, and extra seating arrangements. You also coordinate with your team to be ready for any last-minute surprises. This proactive approach to risk management ensures that the wedding day is as smooth and memorable as possible, despite any unexpected hiccups.

In business, adopting this mindset means identifying potential risks early on, creating strategies to mitigate them, and ensuring all team members are prepared to handle any challenges that arise. This way, an organization can navigate uncertainties and stay on course to achieve its objectives, no matter what surprises come their way.

Risk Identification:

Identifying risks is the crucial first step in managing uncertainties that could harm a company. In a hybrid work setup, these uncertainties can take various forms—like cybersecurity threats in digital spaces, breakdowns in communication during virtual interactions, or disruptions in operations.

Imagine you're overseeing risk management for a global financial institution. One day, you receive a report warning about a possible cyberattack aimed at the organization's online banking platform. This platform is vital because millions of customers rely on it for secure financial transactions.

Your job is to protect the organization's assets and reputation, especially against cybersecurity threats. You immediately gather detailed information about the threat from the IT security team. They provide technical details about how the attack might happen, what vulnerabilities it could exploit, and how it could affect the organization's systems and data. With this information, you assess how serious the threat is and what its potential impact could be.

Using advanced tools that detect threats, you scan the organization's network thoroughly. Your goal is to spot any signs of compromise, like suspicious activities or attempts to access systems without permission. At the same time, you review the organization's existing security measures to find any gaps or weaknesses that attackers could exploit.

Based on your assessment, you create a detailed plan to reduce the risks identified and make the organization stronger against potential cyberattacks. This plan includes technical steps such as fixing vulnerabilities in software, improving security settings, and setting up systems that can detect intrusions. It also involves practical steps like making access controls stricter and teaching employees how to recognize and respond to security threats.

Throughout this process, you keep everyone involved—senior managers, IT staff, and outside cybersecurity experts—informed about the threat and the steps being taken to deal with it. This ensures everyone understands the seriousness of the threat and agrees on what needs to be done. You also keep watch for any new threats or changes in the situation that could affect the organization's security.

Your proactive approach in identifying and dealing with the cyberattack risk shows how important good risk management is in protecting a company's assets and reputation. By acting quickly and decisively to reduce the risk, you help protect the organization's customers, data, and financial health.

Risk Assessment:

Assessing risks involves carefully evaluating their potential impact and likelihood, navigating through uncertainty with precision. This process combines qualitative and quantitative analysis, blending subjective judgment with objective data to understand the magnitude of each risk.

Consider you're overseeing risk management for a manufacturing company heavily reliant on a single supplier for a crucial component in its production process. The company's ability to maintain production schedules and profitability hinges significantly on the timely and consistent delivery of this component. However, you recognize that relying solely on one supplier poses a substantial risk to the company's operations.

To navigate this uncertainty, you conduct a thorough risk assessment. Your goal is to gauge the potential impact of any disruptions from the supplier on production schedules and profitability. This involves analyzing various factors, such as the likelihood of supplier disruptions (like financial instability, labor strikes, or natural disasters), the potential duration of such disruptions, and the financial and operational consequences for your company.

Begin by gathering pertinent data about the supplier's financial health, operational stability, and past track record of reliability. Additionally, consider external factors such as market dynamics, geopolitical risks, and industry regulations that could affect the supplier's ability to fulfill orders. With this information, assess the likelihood of disruptions occurring and the potential severity of their impact on your company's operations.

Next, delve into your supply chain vulnerabilities, identifying potential weak points and critical dependencies. Map out the key suppliers and subcontractors in your supply chain network, pinpointing those whose failure could cascade into broader operational disruptions for your company. Evaluate your supply chain's resilience, looking at factors like redundancy, flexibility, and adaptability to mitigate the risks posed by disruptions.

By conducting this comprehensive risk assessment, you equip yourself with the insights needed to proactively manage and mitigate potential risks to your company's operations. This proactive approach not only helps safeguard production schedules and profitability but also strengthens your company's resilience in the face of uncertainty.

Risk Mitigation:

With risks mapped, it's time to build fortresses against incoming tides of uncertainty. Risk mitigation involves developing strategies to reduce or eliminate risk impact, erecting barriers and safeguards to protect the organization.

Considering you a risk manager in the manufacturing company, based on your risk assessment findings, you develop contingency plans to mitigate the risk of supply chain disruptions. These plans may include:

1. Diversifying Suppliers: One option is to diversify your supplier base by identifying alternative sources of supply for the critical component. This could involve sourcing from multiple suppliers located in different geographic regions to reduce the risk of disruptions caused by localized events.

2. Stockpiling Inventory: Another option is to stockpile inventory of the critical component to buffer against potential supply shortages. By maintaining a strategic inventory reserve, you can ensure continuity of production in the event of supplier disruptions or delays.

3. Negotiating Contracts: You may also negotiate contractual agreements with your suppliers to include provisions for business continuity planning, supply chain resilience, and penalty clauses for non-performance. These contracts can help incentivize suppliers to prioritize your orders and maintain reliable supply chains.

4. Implementing Risk Mitigation Measures: Additionally, you may implement risk mitigation measures such as implementing robust quality control processes, conducting regular supplier audits, and investing in technology

solutions to improve supply chain visibility and resilience.

Consider another scenario. You're the risk manager for a technology startup preparing to launch a new product. Aware of the risk of product defects and customer dissatisfaction, you implement rigorous quality control measures throughout the product development process. You conduct thorough testing at each stage of production, identify and address potential defects early, and provide comprehensive training to customer support staff to handle any issues that may arise post-launch.

Risk Monitoring:

Our journey continues with constant vigilance and monitoring to ensure we stay on course. Risk monitoring uses data and insights as guiding stars, helping us steer clear of hazards and seize opportunities.

Let's look at a scenario where you're the risk manager for a retail chain with stores across the country. With the holiday season fast approaching, concerns about inventory shortages due to increased demand are paramount. The holiday season is crucial for retail sales, and any disruptions to inventory availability could result in lost sales, decreased customer satisfaction, and damage to the brand's reputation.

To navigate this risk effectively, you adopt a proactive approach to risk monitoring, using real-time sales data and inventory tracking systems as your guiding stars. These tools provide valuable insights into product sales trends, stock levels, and customer demand patterns, allowing you to anticipate potential inventory shortages before they occur.

As the holiday season approaches, you closely monitor product sales and stock levels across all store locations in real-time. You analyze sales data to identify which products are selling well and which are experiencing slower-than-expected demand. You also track inventory levels to ensure that sufficient stock is available to meet customer demand during peak shopping periods.

Using this information, you adjust ordering schedules and distribution routes as needed to ensure adequate supply in all locations. For example, if sales of a particular product are outpacing expectations in a specific region, you increase orders to replenish stock levels and prevent shortages. Conversely, if sales of another product are slower than anticipated, you adjust orders accordingly to avoid overstocking and minimize inventory carrying costs.

Your proactive approach to risk monitoring pays off, and the holiday season passes without any major inventory issues. By staying vigilant and responsive to changes in customer demand and market conditions, you ensure that your retail chain can meet the needs of holiday shoppers and capitalize on sales opportunities during this critical period.

Agile Risk Management:

Traditional approaches to risk management can often be too rigid for dynamic environments. Agile risk management offers the adaptability and responsiveness needed to effectively navigate hybrid work environments.

Let's delve into an example involving a software development company transitioning to a remote work model. The shift to remote work raises concerns about potential risks like decreased productivity and communication breakdowns. To address these challenges, you decide to implement agile risk management practices that emphasize flexibility and continuous improvement.

You start by introducing daily stand-up meetings, where team members briefly share their progress, challenges, and plans for the day. These meetings, held at the same time each morning, provide an opportunity for the team to stay aligned and address any obstacles quickly. This practice ensures everyone is on the same page and that any issues are identified and resolved promptly.

Next, you organize weekly sprint planning sessions. During these sessions, the team reviews their progress from the previous week, discusses priorities, and plans their tasks for the upcoming week. By breaking down the project into manageable chunks, or "sprints," the team can focus on delivering small, incremental improvements. This approach not only makes the project more manageable but also allows the team to adapt to changes and new requirements as they arise.

In addition to daily stand-ups and weekly planning, you hold regular retrospectives. These are reflective meetings where the team discusses what went well, what didn't, and how they can improve their processes. Retrospectives encourage open and honest communication, enabling the team to learn from their experiences and continuously enhance their ways of working. This iterative process of reflection and improvement is a cornerstone of agile risk management.

To support these agile practices, you also implement tools and technologies that facilitate remote collaboration. Project management software, like Jira or Trello, helps the team track their tasks and progress. Communication platforms, such as Slack or Microsoft Teams, provide channels for instant messaging and video conferencing, ensuring that team members can easily communicate and collaborate, regardless of their location.

Through these agile practices, your team can quickly respond to changes and uncertainties. If a team member encounters a roadblock, it can be addressed immediately during a stand-up meeting. If priorities shift due to client feedback or market changes, the team can adjust their plans during the next sprint planning session. The regular cadence of retrospectives ensures that the team is always learning and improving, making them more resilient to future challenges.

As a result, your software development company successfully navigates the transition to remote work. The team remains productive, communication channels are robust, and projects are delivered on time and within budget. By embracing agile risk management, you've created an environment that thrives on flexibility and continuous improvement, enabling your organization to adapt and succeed in a dynamic hybrid work environment.

Chapter 2

IDENTIFYING THE UNKNOWNS

"The biggest risk is not taking any risk. In a world that's changing really quickly, the only strategy that is guaranteed to fail is not taking risks."

— Mark Zuckerberg

Challenges in a Hybrid Work Setting

The role of a risk manager has transformed significantly in the hybrid work environment, presenting a blend of opportunities and challenges. Starting your day involves reviewing risk reports generated overnight. These reports act as your early warning system, bringing potential issues to light before they escalate. With your team distributed across various locations, maintaining effective communication becomes essential.

Your daily responsibilities are varied and dynamic. You might begin your day with a virtual stand-up meeting, a quick and efficient way to synchronize on tasks, share updates, and highlight any immediate risks. This practice, borrowed from agile methodologies, ensures that everyone understands their role and is aware of any new developments. Let's explore four of the most common responsibilities of a risk manager across several domains.

Functional Key Responsibilities:

1. Monitoring Risks:

As a risk manager, your day-to-day tasks involve using various tools and dashboards that continuously provide data on emerging threats and vulnerabilities. For instance, you might notice an unusual spike in network traffic, which could signal a potential cyberattack. Your job then becomes similar to that of a detective, where you must analyze the data, identify patterns, and spot signs of trouble to prevent a disaster.

Let's consider a different example to make this clearer. Suppose you are the risk manager for a global e-commerce company. One day, you receive a report indicating a potential cyberattack targeting your company's website. This platform is crucial, as millions of customers rely on it for their online shopping needs, and any disruption could lead to significant financial losses and damage to your company's reputation.

To tackle this, you use advanced threat detection tools, such as SIEM (Security Information and Event Management) systems, which help you monitor and analyze security events in real-time. Additionally, you conduct thorough security audits using vulnerability scanners like Nessus or Qualys to identify weaknesses in your system.

Once vulnerabilities are identified, you implement robust security measures. These could include multi-factor authentication (MFA) to ensure that users must provide two or more verification factors to gain access, end-to-end encryption to protect data from being read or modified by anyone other than the sender and receiver, and regular penetration testing to simulate cyberattacks and identify security gaps.

By combining these tools and strategies, you effectively

mitigate the risk of a cyberattack, ensuring the safety and reliability of your e-commerce platform. This proactive approach not only protects the company's assets but also maintains the trust and confidence of your customers, ensuring that their shopping experience remains secure and uninterrupted.

2. Communicating with Stakeholders:

Clear communication is the backbone of effective risk management. Ensuring all stakeholders, including remote team members, are informed about potential risks and mitigation strategies is essential. This might involve sending detailed reports, hosting virtual meetings, or using collaboration tools to keep information flowing smoothly.

For example, let's say you are the risk manager for a large healthcare organization. The organization is planning a significant upgrade to its electronic health records (EHR) system. This upgrade is crucial for improving patient care, but it also poses substantial risks if not managed correctly.

To manage this risk, you maintain constant communication with the IT team, healthcare providers, project managers, and executive leadership. You start by sending detailed reports that outline potential risks, such as data breaches, system downtime, and compliance issues. These reports also include the mitigation strategies that will be implemented to address these risks.

In addition to reports, you host regular virtual meetings to discuss progress and address any concerns. These meetings are attended by key stakeholders, ensuring that everyone is on the same page and can provide input on the risk management plan. You use collaboration tools like Slack for real-time messaging, Confluence for documentation, and Zoom for video conferencing to facilitate these discussions.

By keeping communication channels open and effective, you ensure that all stakeholders are aware of the potential risks and the steps being taken to mitigate them. This proactive approach helps in aligning everyone's expectations and preempting any potential issues, ultimately ensuring a smooth and successful system upgrade.

Clear communication helps build trust and ensures that all team members are aligned, which is crucial for the success of any project. In the healthcare example, it helps in managing the complexities of a system upgrade, ensuring that the transition is seamless and that patient care is not compromised.

3. Implementing Mitigation Strategies:

When a risk is identified, quick action is essential. Suppose you discover a cybersecurity threat. You'd immediately coordinate with the IT team to bolster defenses, conduct system checks, and update protocols. Your role is to bring together different departments to tackle risks efficiently.

Alternatively, consider you are the risk manager for a tech startup heavily reliant on cloud services. One day, you receive alerts of potential service disruptions from your cloud service provider due to network issues. This situation threatens to disrupt your operations, affecting product development timelines and customer satisfaction.

In response, you swiftly engage with the IT team and other relevant stakeholders to assess the situation. Using monitoring tools like CloudHealth and AWS CloudWatch, you gather real-time data on service availability and performance metrics. This information helps you understand the extent of the potential disruption and its impact on your business operations.

Based on your assessment, you implement mitigation strategies such as activating redundant cloud service instances across multiple regions, ensuring failover mechanisms are in place, and increasing bandwidth capacity to handle potential spikes in traffic. These proactive measures help mitigate the risk of service disruptions and ensure continuity of operations for your startup.

Additionally, you collaborate with your cloud service provider to review their incident response and disaster recovery plans. This partnership allows you to align on communication protocols and escalation procedures, ensuring swift resolution and minimal impact on your business.

By taking decisive action and leveraging technology tools, you demonstrate effective risk management in navigating disruptions to cloud services. Your proactive approach ensures that your startup can maintain operational resilience and continue delivering products and services to customers without interruption.

4. Training and Awareness:

Ensuring your team is well-prepared to manage risks effectively is crucial for the security of your organization. Regular training sessions play a vital role in equipping everyone with the knowledge and skills needed to identify and mitigate potential risks. For instance, hosting webinars or workshops where employees learn how to recognize phishing emails and other common security threats can significantly enhance their awareness.

Consider conducting a series of training sessions focused on data security using a platform like KnowBe4. These sessions cover essential topics such as best practices for handling sensitive information, recognizing suspicious activities, and understanding cybersecurity protocols. As a result of these initiatives, employees become more vigilant and capable of identifying potential threats before they escalate.

This proactive approach not only strengthens your organization's defense against cyber threats but also empowers employees to play an active role in safeguarding company assets. By ensuring that everyone understands risk management protocols through effective training, you cultivate a workforce that is informed, prepared, and capable of responding effectively to security challenges. This ultimately contributes to maintaining a secure and resilient environment for your organization's operations.

Most common Challenges of a Risk Manager:

1. **Cybersecurity Threats:** As a risk manager, you face several key challenges in today's dynamic work environment. One of the foremost concerns is cybersecurity threats. As businesses adopt hybrid work setups, the risk of cyberattacks has increased. This means protecting sensitive data and systems from hackers is a constant priority. Regularly monitoring network activities, keeping software up-to-date, and implementing strong security measures are essential defenses against such threats.

For example, let's look at a retail chain preparing for the busy holiday season. The risk manager here is worried about potential inventory shortages due to higher customer demand. To tackle this risk effectively, they use advanced tools like

Oracle NetSuite for real-time tracking of product sales and stock levels across all stores. By closely monitoring these metrics, they can adjust their ordering schedules and distribution strategies as needed. This proactive approach ensures that the retail chain can meet customer demands without running into major inventory problems during the holiday rush.

Navigating these challenges requires staying vigilant, leveraging technology for real-time insights, and taking proactive steps to mitigate risks before they escalate. By addressing these challenges head-on, risk managers play a crucial role in safeguarding their organizations' operations and maintaining resilience in the face of evolving threats and uncertainties.

2. **Operational Disruptions:** Ensuring smooth operations can be challenging when your team is spread across different locations. It requires effective contingency planning and leveraging appropriate tools.

For instance, consider a scenario where you're overseeing risk management for a tech company with a global workforce. Suddenly, a power outage hits one region, disrupting operations. However, due to your well-prepared contingency plan, which includes backup power solutions and decentralized workflows using tools like Git for version control and AWS for cloud services, the impact of the disruption is minimal. Critical projects can continue without significant delays.

In such situations, having robust contingency plans in place and using cloud-based project management systems like Asana or Jira can facilitate real-time collaboration, ensuring projects stay on track even amidst unexpected challenges. This proactive approach helps mitigate operational disruptions and keeps the organization agile and responsive across different geographical locations.

3. **Communication Gaps:** Clear and consistent communication is crucial in a hybrid work environment but can be challenging to maintain. Establishing robust communication channels is essential to keep teams connected and projects running smoothly.

Imagine managing a large-scale project with team members spread across various time zones. To overcome communication challenges, you utilize tools like Slack for instant messaging, Trello for task management, and Microsoft Teams for video calls. These platforms enable real-time communication and collaboration, ensuring everyone is informed and engaged regardless of their location. By bridging the gap between remote and in-office teams, this seamless communication network helps prevent misunderstandings and ensures the project stays on track.

In a hybrid work setting, where remote work and digital

interactions are prevalent, effective communication tools and practices play a pivotal role in fostering collaboration and maintaining productivity across distributed teams.

Working in a hybrid environment requires a flexible and adaptive approach, and this is where agile methodologies come into play. These methodologies emphasize flexibility, teamwork, and continuous improvement, allowing teams to quickly adjust to changes and stay on course.

Agile methodologies involve practices like daily stand-up meetings, where team members briefly share updates on their tasks, any obstacles they're facing, and what they'll work on next. This helps keep everyone informed and aligned. Tools like Trello or Jira are essential in managing projects efficiently. They help you track tasks, assign responsibilities, and monitor progress in real-time. Open communication is another crucial aspect, ensuring that all team members can easily share information and collaborate effectively, regardless of where they're working from.

Navigating the Daily Life of a Risk Manager in a Hybrid Setting

The daily life of a risk manager in a hybrid work environment is dynamic and demands a proactive approach. Each day starts with reviewing the latest data and risk reports to identify any new threats or vulnerabilities. Staying ahead of potential issues requires constant vigilance and the ability to quickly analyze and respond to emerging risks.

Using advanced tools is part of your everyday routine. Real-time monitoring systems help you keep track of various risk factors, while project management platforms like Trello or Jira streamline task management and ensure that everyone is on the same page. Regular communication through instant messaging, video calls, and collaborative tools keeps the team connected and informed.

Agile methods are at the heart of your strategy. By holding daily stand-up meetings, you ensure that the team remains focused and can quickly address any issues that arise. Continuous feedback loops and regular retrospectives help the team learn from each project and improve processes for the future.

The Importance of Your Role

As a risk manager, your role is crucial in guiding the organization through the complexities of hybrid work. Your ability to anticipate risks, implement effective mitigation strategies, and maintain clear communication channels helps the organization remain resilient. By adopting agile methodologies and leveraging advanced tools, you can navigate the challenges of hybrid work and ensure that your organization is well-prepared to adapt and respond to any situation that arises.

Your proactive approach not only protects the organization from potential risks but also contributes to a culture of continuous improvement and collaboration. In these uncertain times, your leadership and expertise are vital in steering the organization towards success, ready to tackle new challenges with confidence.

Chapter 3

ASSESS, MITIGATE, MONITOR

"It is better to be roughly right than precisely wrong."

— *John Maynard Keynes*

Effective Communication Techniques

Managing global stakeholders in a hybrid work environment requires careful coordination and strategic communication. In this setting, the role of a risk manager extends beyond traditional boundaries.

For example, you might need to organize a risk management meeting at 8 AM in New York while a colleague in Tokyo is preparing for bed. This situation highlights the importance of effective communication that goes beyond just exchanging information; it involves connecting across different time zones, cultures, and communication styles.

To achieve this, use a variety of tools and strategies. Instant messaging platforms can facilitate quick updates and real-time communication. Video calls are essential for face-to-face interactions, which help build rapport and ensure clear understanding. Regular check-ins help maintain a steady flow of information and keep everyone aligned.

Adapting your communication methods to suit different preferences is also crucial. For instance, some stakeholders might prefer detailed emails, while others might favor brief, direct messages. Being mindful of time zone differences and scheduling meetings at mutually convenient times can help in accommodating everyone's availability. Understanding cultural nuances and communication styles can further enhance your effectiveness in managing global stakeholders.

By using these techniques, you can ensure that your communication is clear, inclusive, and effective, helping to keep all stakeholders engaged and informed, regardless of their location.

Strategies for Managing Global Stakeholders:

Managing global stakeholders effectively involves keeping them informed and engaged. Here are four common strategies to achieve this, along with their core principles, strengths, and practical solutions to overcome their limitations.

1. Regular Updates:

Providing regular updates is crucial for building trust and maintaining transparency with stakeholders. These updates should be clear, concise, and consistent, offering valuable insights into risk management activities and any incidents that occur.

Core Principles and Structure:

- **Schedule Regular Updates:** Decide on a regular update schedule, whether weekly, bi-weekly, or monthly, to ensure stakeholders are consistently informed.

- **Focus on Key Developments:** Highlight important progress in risk mitigation efforts and any new risks identified. Use both qualitative and quantitative data.
- **Use Multiple Communication Channels:** Mix communication methods, such as emails, newsletters, video conferences, and project management platforms.

Think of starting your Monday with a clear, well-structured update from your team lead, detailing last week's achievements and this week's goals. This practice builds a sense of rhythm and trust. Whether it's an email bulletin or a brief video update, keeping everyone informed helps create a cohesive team spirit, even when working from different locations.

Pfizer, a global pharmaceutical company, uses regular updates to keep its diverse group of stakeholders informed about the latest developments in drug research and production risks. By providing weekly updates through email newsletters and quarterly video conferences, Pfizer ensures all stakeholders, from regulatory bodies to investors, are aligned and informed.

Strengths and Solutions by Pfizer:

Pfizer provided regular updates to build trust and transparency, keeping stakeholders engaged and informed. It helped in early identification of issues. To avoid overloading stakeholders with information, they streamlined the update process by using templates and automating reports wherever possible. Task delegation to distribute the workload efficiently worked well in several situations.

By implementing these strategies, you also can manage global stakeholders more effectively, ensuring clear communication and a well-informed, cohesive team.

2. Cultural Sensitivity:

Understanding and respecting cultural differences is essential when managing global stakeholders. Different cultures have unique communication styles, decision-making processes, and business etiquettes.

Core Principles and Structure:

- **Educate Yourself and Your Team:** Learn about the cultural backgrounds of your stakeholders. This knowledge helps you understand their communication styles and preferences.
- **Tailor Your Communication Style:** Adapt your communication to fit the cultural preferences of your stakeholders. For example, some cultures prefer direct communication, while others value a more indirect approach.
- **Show Respect for Cultural Norms:** Use appropriate titles and observe local customs when interacting with stakeholders. This shows respect and helps build strong

relationships.

You're on a video call with stakeholders from different continents. Your Asian colleagues might prefer a more indirect communication style, while your European partners appreciate directness. Being aware of these preferences helps you communicate more effectively, turning potentially awkward interactions into respectful and productive discussions.

Unilever, a global company, adapts its communication strategies to fit local markets. In Asia, Unilever teams use more formal communication and respect hierarchical structures. In North America, they adopt a more casual and direct approach.

Strengths and Solutions by Unilever:

- **Strength**: Unilever's cultural sensitivity fosters stronger relationships with stakeholders and reduces misunderstandings.
    - **Solution**: By continuously educating their teams on cultural differences, Unilever ensures effective communication and collaboration.
- **Strength**: Unilever's approach helps prevent potential conflicts and enhances stakeholder engagement.
    - **Solution**: They invest in cultural sensitivity training for their teams and provide resources like cultural guides and workshops.

- **Strength**: Unilever avoids missteps in communication by understanding cultural nuances.
  - **Solution**: They engage with local experts or cultural advisors to provide insights and guidance.
- **Strength**: Regular reviews of communication strategies ensure they remain culturally appropriate.
  - **Solution**: Unilever conducts regular assessments of their communication practices to align with cultural expectations and norms.

By understanding and respecting cultural differences, Unilever builds stronger relationships with global stakeholders and navigates potential challenges more effectively.

3. Collaborative Tools:

In a hybrid work environment, using collaborative tools is essential for smooth communication and information sharing. These tools help bridge the gap between remote and in-office teams, making it easier to work together.

Core Principles and Structure:

- **Select Appropriate Tools**: Choose tools that meet the specific needs of your team and stakeholders. Examples include Slack for instant messaging, Microsoft Teams for video conferencing, and Asana for project management.

- **Integrate Tools into Workflows:** Ensure that these tools are part of your daily work routines and that all team members know how to use them effectively.
- **Ensure Accessibility:** Make sure that the tools are accessible to all stakeholders, regardless of their location or technical proficiency.

Imagine you're the risk manager for a healthcare company coordinating a project with team members spread across different cities. You decide to use a combination of Slack for instant messaging, Microsoft Teams for video calls, and Trello for project management.

Using Collaborative Tools Effectively:

Select Appropriate Tools: You choose Slack because it allows for quick communication and easy sharing of documents. Microsoft Teams is chosen for its reliable video conferencing capabilities, and Trello for its visual project management features.

Integrate Tools into Workflows: You make these tools a part of your team's daily activities. Every morning, team members check Trello for their tasks, use Slack throughout the day for quick questions and updates, and join weekly project meetings on Microsoft Teams.

Ensure Accessibility: To ensure everyone can use these tools effectively, you provide training sessions and user guides. You also set up a support system where team members can ask for help if they encounter any issues.

A company like **Bayer**, which operates in the pharmaceutical industry, uses collaborative tools to manage its global operations. Bayer uses Microsoft Teams for video meetings, Slack for real-time communication, and Trello to keep track of project progress. These tools ensure that all team members and stakeholders are well-informed and coordinated, no matter where they are located.

Strengths and Solutions by Bayer:

- **Strength**: Bayer's use of collaborative tools ensures that everyone is on the same page, reducing misunderstandings and improving efficiency.
    - **Solution**: By integrating these tools into their daily workflows and providing training, Bayer ensures that all team members can use them effectively.
- **Strength:** The tools facilitate real-time communication and collaboration, making it easier to solve problems quickly.
    - **Solution**: Bayer offers ongoing support and backup communication channels to handle any technical issues that might arise.
- **Strength**: Collaborative tools help Bayer manage its global

workforce and keep projects on track.

- **Solution**: Regular training and comprehensive user guides ensure that all employees are proficient in using the tools.

By effectively using collaborative tools, Bayer can maintain smooth communication and coordination across its global teams, ensuring that projects are completed efficiently and on time.

4. Feedback Mechanisms:

Creating channels for stakeholders to provide feedback is vital for spotting potential issues early and promoting a collaborative approach to risk management. Feedback mechanisms should be easy to use and encourage open communication.

Core Principles and Structure:

- **Set Up Multiple Feedback Channels:** Implement various methods for gathering feedback, such as surveys, digital suggestion boxes, dedicated email addresses, and regular feedback meetings.
- **Encourage Honest Feedback:** Ensure confidentiality and demonstrate a commitment to acting on feedback to encourage stakeholders to share their honest and constructive opinions.
- **Regularly Review and Act on Feedback:** Regularly go through the feedback received and update stakeholders on

the actions taken in response to their input.

Imagine you're the risk manager for a global consumer goods company. To gather feedback from employees and stakeholders, you set up a digital platform where they can submit their ideas and concerns anonymously at any time. Additionally, you conduct quarterly surveys and organize bi-monthly feedback meetings.

Implementing Feedback Mechanisms Effectively:

Set Up Multiple Feedback Channels: You create an online portal for anonymous feedback submissions, distribute quarterly surveys to gather structured input, and hold bi-monthly meetings to discuss feedback openly.

Encourage Honest Feedback: You assure all participants that their feedback is confidential and will be taken seriously. This encourages more people to share their thoughts without fear of repercussions.

Regularly Review and Act on Feedback: You and your team review the feedback on a weekly basis, identifying common themes and areas for improvement. You then communicate the actions taken based on this feedback in monthly newsletters to keep everyone informed.

A company like **Procter & Gamble (P&G)**, known for its

strong focus on innovation and employee engagement, uses feedback mechanisms effectively. P&G employs regular employee surveys, digital suggestion boxes, and open forums to gather input from its workforce and other stakeholders. This feedback is then analyzed and integrated into their continuous improvement processes.

Strengths and Solutions by P&G:

- **Strength**: P&G's feedback mechanisms ensure that valuable insights from employees and stakeholders are captured and acted upon.
  - **Solution**: By setting up diverse feedback channels and encouraging honest input, P&G ensures a steady flow of valuable information.
- **Strength**: Regularly reviewing and acting on feedback fosters a culture of continuous improvement.
  - **Solution**: P&G dedicates resources to manage the feedback process efficiently, using automated tools to collect and analyze data.
- **Strength**: Effective handling of feedback, including negative input, promotes a constructive and open company culture.
  - **Solution**: P&G trains managers to view negative feedback as opportunities for growth, ensuring that all feedback is addressed constructively.

By adopting these feedback mechanisms, Procter & Gamble

effectively manages stakeholder relationships and continuously improves its processes. This approach ensures that communication remains open and productive, fostering a collaborative environment where every stakeholder's voice is heard.

Chapter 4

NAVIGATING DAILY CHALLENGES

"In preparing for battle I have always found that plans are useless, but planning is indispensable."

— *Dwight D. Eisenhower*

Exploring Risk Management Frameworks

Understanding and managing risks in a hybrid work environment can be complex. To handle this effectively, organizations use strategic and adaptable approaches called risk management frameworks. These frameworks help identify, assess, and mitigate risks. In this chapter, we will look at some popular risk management frameworks, discuss their main ideas, and see how they are used in real-world scenarios.

COSO (Committee of Sponsoring Organizations) ERM Framework:

The COSO Enterprise Risk Management (ERM) Framework is designed to help organizations manage risks in a structured and integrated way. Here's a detailed look at how it works, along with a real-world example from JP Morgan & Chase.

Core Principles and Structure of COSO ERM:

- **Governance and Culture:** Establishes the tone at the top, promoting a culture that is aware of risks throughout the organization.
- **Strategy and Objective-Setting:** Aligns risk management with the organization's goals.
- **Performance:** Involves identifying and assessing risks that could impact the organization.
- **Review and Revision:** Ensures that risk management practices are continuously monitored and updated.
- **Information, Communication, and Reporting:** Guarantees timely and transparent communication of risk-related information.

JP Morgan & Chase Example:

Governance and Culture: JP Morgan & Chase established a

dedicated risk management committee at the executive level to set the tone for risk management. This committee includes senior leaders from different departments who ensure that a risk-aware culture is promoted throughout the organization. They conduct regular training sessions and workshops to educate employees about the importance of risk management and how it aligns with the bank's goals.

Strategy and Objective-Setting: When JP Morgan & Chase sets its strategic objectives, risk management is a key component. For example, when planning to expand its operations into new markets, the bank conducts a thorough risk assessment to identify potential political, economic, and operational risks. They then develop strategies to mitigate these risks, such as diversifying investments and establishing strong local partnerships.

Performance: The bank uses sophisticated tools and technologies to identify and assess risks. For instance, they employ advanced data analytics to monitor market trends and detect early signs of financial instability. This allows them to take proactive measures, such as adjusting their investment portfolios or implementing stricter lending criteria to safeguard against potential losses.

Review and Revision: JP Morgan & Chase has a robust

process for regularly reviewing and updating its risk management practices. They conduct quarterly risk assessments and audits to ensure that their risk management strategies are effective and up-to-date. Any identified gaps or weaknesses are addressed promptly, and the risk management framework is revised accordingly to adapt to new challenges.

Information, Communication, and Reporting: To ensure timely and transparent communication, JP Morgan & Chase has implemented a comprehensive reporting system. They use dashboards and real-time reporting tools to keep stakeholders informed about potential risks and mitigation efforts. Regular updates are shared through email newsletters, video conferences, and dedicated risk management portals accessible to all employees and key stakeholders.

Strengths of the COSO ERM Framework:

- **Comprehensive and Integrated:** Covers all aspects of risk management and ensures they are part of the overall strategy.
- **Encourages a Risk-Aware Culture:** Everyone in the organization becomes aware of risks and how to handle them.

Challenges and Solutions:

- **Complex to Implement:** Can be difficult, especially for smaller organizations.
- **Phased Approach:** Start by integrating the framework into different parts of the organization step by step.
- **External Consultants:** Hiring experts to help with the initial setup and training can make the process smoother.

In summary, JP Morgan & Chase effectively uses the COSO ERM Framework to manage risks by aligning risk management with their strategic goals and promoting a culture that is aware of risks. By establishing strong governance, continuously monitoring and updating risk practices, and ensuring clear communication, they mitigate potential risks and safeguard their operations.

ISO 31000

The International Organization for Standardization (ISO) 31000 provides guidelines and principles for risk management that can be used by any organization, no matter its size, industry, or sector. Here's how it works and a real-world example to help explain.

Core Principles and Structure of ISO 31000:

Risk Assessment: Identifying and analyzing potential risks that could affect the organization.

Risk Treatment: Developing strategies to manage and mitigate those risks.

Monitoring and Review: Continuously checking and updating risk management practices to ensure they are effective.

Implementation: Applying risk management practices throughout the organization to ensure everyone is aware and involved.

Siemens Example:

Risk Assessment: Siemens, a global technology company, uses ISO 31000 to assess risks in its various business units. For example, in their renewable energy division, they identify potential risks like supply chain disruptions, regulatory changes, and technological failures. They analyze these risks to understand their potential impact on the business.

Risk Treatment: After identifying risks, Siemens develops strategies to manage them. For supply chain risks, they might diversify their suppliers to ensure they are not overly dependent on one source. For regulatory changes, they keep a close watch on new laws and regulations in the countries they operate in and adjust their operations accordingly. For technological failures, they invest in research and development to continuously improve their products.

Monitoring and Review: Siemens doesn't just set and forget their risk management strategies. They continuously monitor the effectiveness of their risk treatments and make adjustments as necessary. For example, if a supplier starts to show signs of instability, they might increase orders from alternative suppliers to mitigate any potential disruption.

Implementation: ISO 31000 principles are applied across all levels of Siemens. This means that from the top executives to the front-line employees, everyone is aware of the risks and the strategies in place to manage them. They use standardized processes to ensure that risk management is consistent across all business units and locations.

Strengths of ISO 31000:

Universal Applicability: It can be used by any organization, no matter its industry or size.

Emphasis on Creating and Protecting Value: Ensures that risk management efforts contribute to the organization's success.

Challenges and Solutions:

- **Generic Nature:** While ISO 31000 is designed to be applicable to any organization, its broad guidelines may need to be customized to fit specific organizational needs.
- **Tailoring to Specific Contexts:** Organizations should adapt the principles and processes to their specific situations. Siemens, for example, develops detailed guidelines for each of its business units to ensure that risk management practices are relevant and effective.
- **Sector-Specific Guidelines:** In addition to the general ISO framework, Siemens creates specific guidelines for different sectors, like healthcare, energy, and industry, to address unique risks in each area.

In summary, Siemens uses ISO 31000 to effectively manage risks across its diverse operations by standardizing risk management practices, continuously monitoring and updating their strategies, and tailoring the framework to fit specific needs. This helps Siemens stay resilient and prepared for any challenges that come their way.

NIST Risk Management Framework:

The National Institute of Standards and Technology (NIST) Risk Management Framework (RMF) is a set of guidelines primarily used by U.S. federal agencies and organizations that need to follow strict cybersecurity standards. Here's a breakdown of its core principles and a practical example to explain how it works.

Core Principles and Structure of NIST RMF:

- **Categorize Information and Systems:** Identify and classify the information and systems that need protection based on their importance and sensitivity.
- **Select Security Controls:** Choose appropriate security measures to protect these information systems.
- **Implement Security Controls:** Put the selected security measures into action.
- **Assess Effectiveness:** Evaluate how well the security measures are working.
- **Authorize System Operation:** Approve the system for use based on the assessment results.
- **Continuous Monitoring:** Keep an ongoing watch on the security of the system to ensure it remains effective and address new threats as they arise.

Lockheed Martin Example:

Lockheed Martin, a major defense contractor, uses the NIST RMF to secure its information systems. Here's how they apply this framework:

Categorize Information and Systems: Lockheed Martin starts by identifying all the types of information they handle, such as classified defense data and sensitive project details. They categorize these based on how critical and sensitive they are, deciding what needs the most protection.

Select Security Controls: Next, they choose security measures suitable for protecting their categorized information. For highly sensitive data, this might include advanced encryption, multi-factor authentication, and strict access controls.

Implement Security Controls: Lockheed Martin then implements these security measures across their systems. This involves setting up encryption protocols, configuring firewalls, and ensuring that only authorized personnel can access critical data.

Assess Effectiveness: They continuously test these security measures to see how well they are working. This might involve running simulated cyberattacks to identify any weaknesses and ensure the measures are robust enough to withstand real threats.

Authorize System Operation: Based on the assessments, Lockheed Martin decides if the systems are secure enough to be used. If any issues are found during testing, they must be resolved before the systems are authorized for operation.

Continuous Monitoring: Even after the systems are up and running, Lockheed Martin keeps monitoring them to spot any new vulnerabilities or threats. They use real-time monitoring tools and regularly review security protocols to keep their defenses strong.

Strengths of NIST RMF:

- **Rigorous and Detailed Approach:** Provides a thorough process for ensuring cybersecurity, aligning with federal standards.
- **Structured and Systematic:** Offers clear steps to follow, making it easier to manage and secure information systems.

Challenges and Solutions:

- **Specificity to Cybersecurity and U.S. Federal Requirements:** NIST RMF is primarily focused on cybersecurity and U.S. federal needs, which might not cover all types of risks an organization faces.
- **Integration with Other Frameworks:** To address this, Lockheed Martin integrates NIST RMF with other risk

management frameworks that handle non-cyber risks. For instance, they might combine it with the ISO 31000 framework to manage broader operational and strategic risks.

- **Adapting to Different Environments:** Lockheed Martin customizes the NIST RMF principles to fit different regulatory environments they operate in, ensuring comprehensive risk management across all areas of their business.

By following the NIST RMF, Lockheed Martin effectively manages cybersecurity risks, ensuring compliance with federal regulations and protecting their critical information systems from potential threats. This detailed and structured approach helps them maintain a strong security posture and respond swiftly to any emerging risks.

FAIR Model:

The Factor Analysis of Information Risk (FAIR) model is a quantitative approach to risk management, especially focused on cybersecurity risks. This model helps organizations analyze and manage risks by translating them into financial terms, making it easier to prioritize and address them.

Core Principles and Structure of the FAIR Model:

- **Identify and Define Risk Scenarios:** Start by identifying specific scenarios that could pose a risk to the organization. This involves detailing what could go wrong, how it could happen, and what the consequences might be.
- **Analyze Risk Factors:** Examine the factors that contribute to these risks. This includes assessing how often threat events might occur (threat event frequency) and the potential severity of their impact (loss magnitude).
- **Quantify Risk in Financial Terms:** Use data and statistical methods to translate these risks into financial terms. This helps to understand the potential cost of risks and to prioritize them based on their financial impact.

Example: How Netflix Uses the FAIR Model:

Identify and Define Risk Scenarios: Netflix begins by identifying various cybersecurity risks that could affect its operations. For example, they might consider the risk of a data breach exposing customer information or a cyberattack disrupting their streaming service.

Analyze Risk Factors: Next, Netflix analyzes the factors that contribute to these risks. They assess how frequently cyberattacks might occur and evaluate the potential financial impact of these events. For instance, they consider the cost of lost revenue if the streaming service is disrupted and the potential fines and damage to reputation if customer data is compromised.

Quantify Risk in Financial Terms: Netflix then translates these risks into financial terms using historical data, industry benchmarks, and statistical methods. This helps them understand the potential financial loss associated with each risk scenario. For example, they might determine that a data breach could cost the company millions of dollars in fines and lost business.

Implementing the FAIR Model: By quantifying the risks in financial terms, Netflix can prioritize their investments in cybersecurity measures. If the analysis shows that a particular risk scenario could result in significant financial loss, they will allocate more resources to mitigate that risk. For instance, they might invest in advanced encryption technologies or hire additional cybersecurity experts.

Strengths of the FAIR Model:

- **Quantitative Approach:** Provides clear and actionable insights by translating technical risks into business terms.
- **Informed Decision-Making:** Helps prioritize risk management efforts based on their potential financial impact, ensuring resources are allocated effectively.

Challenges and Solutions:

- **Data Requirements:** The FAIR model requires accurate and comprehensive data for effective analysis.
- **Robust Data Collection:** To address this, Netflix implements strong data collection and management processes. They use historical data on past security incidents and industry benchmarks to supplement their internal data.
- **Continuous Improvement:** Netflix regularly updates their data and risk scenarios to reflect the latest cybersecurity threats and trends. This ensures that their risk management practices remain relevant and effective.

By using the FAIR model, Netflix can effectively quantify and manage cybersecurity risks, ensuring that their investments in security measures are aligned with the potential financial impact. This approach helps them protect their operations and customer data while maintaining a strong focus on business priorities.

Agile Risk Management Framework:

The Agile Risk Management (ARM) Framework is designed for dynamic environments where risks can change quickly. It focuses on flexibility, teamwork, and adapting rapidly to new challenges.

Core Principles and Structure of ARM Framework:

- **Iterative Processes:** Risk management activities are carried out in short, iterative cycles rather than in a single, comprehensive plan. This allows for quick adjustments as new risks emerge or conditions change.
- **Collaboration:** Teams from different functions work closely together, sharing information and expertise to address risks effectively. This collaboration ensures that everyone is on the same page and can respond swiftly.
- **Continuous Review and Refinement:** Risk management practices are regularly reviewed and improved based on feedback and new information. This ongoing process helps to stay proactive and adaptable.
- **Adaptability:** ARM emphasizes the ability to adapt quickly to new risks and changing conditions, ensuring that responses are timely and effective.

Example: Spotify Using Agile Risk Management:

Iterative Processes: Spotify applies ARM by continuously assessing and managing risks in short cycles. For example, they regularly review user data security and privacy risks to ensure compliance and trust with their subscribers.

Collaboration: Different teams at Spotify, such as software developers and security experts, collaborate closely to address risks. This teamwork helps them to quickly identify vulnerabilities in their systems and implement solutions.

Continuous Improvement: Spotify regularly refines their risk management practices based on user feedback and industry trends. For instance, they may update their encryption protocols or enhance their fraud detection systems to mitigate emerging risks.

Adaptability: When Spotify encounters new technological or market risks, they quickly adjust their strategies. For instance, they might revise their content recommendation algorithms to address new user preferences or enhance their cybersecurity measures in response to evolving threats.

Strengths of ARM Framework:

- **Adaptability and Responsiveness:** ARM allows organizations like Spotify to respond quickly to changes in their environment, minimizing potential disruptions and seizing opportunities.
- **Enhanced Collaboration:** By fostering teamwork across

different departments, ARM ensures that diverse perspectives are considered when managing risks.

Challenges and Solutions:

- **Coordination and Communication:** Effective implementation of ARM requires strong coordination and communication among teams.
- **Collaborative Tools:** Spotify uses tools like Slack for instant messaging and Jira for project management to facilitate communication and alignment.
- **Regular Meetings:** They conduct regular meetings to discuss risk status, actions taken, and upcoming challenges, ensuring everyone understands their roles and responsibilities.

In summary, Spotify enhances its ability to manage risks effectively in a fast-paced industry by employing the Agile Risk Management Framework. This approach not only safeguards their operations but also fosters innovation and growth by adapting swiftly to changing market conditions and technological advancements.

Chapter 5

STAKEHOLDER SYMBIOSIS

"In business, every risk is worth taking as long as it's backed by a sound business plan and a strong sense of ethics."

— Harold S. Geneen

Why are risk management case studies important?

Risk management case studies showcase how organizations identify, assess, and address various risks in real-world scenarios. They provide concrete examples of risk management in action, helping you see how theoretical concepts apply in practical situations. This makes it easier to understand the steps involved in managing risks and the outcomes of different strategies.

Learning from Others' Experiences:

Case studies offer valuable insights into the successes and failures of other organizations. By studying these examples, you can learn what worked well and what didn't. This knowledge helps you avoid common pitfalls and adopt best practices, improving your own risk management efforts.

Enhancing Problem-Solving Skills:

Analyzing case studies requires critical thinking and problem-solving skills. As you review the challenges faced by organizations and the solutions they implemented, you develop your own ability to assess risks and devise effective strategies. This hands-on learning approach strengthens your skills and prepares you for real-life risk management situations.

Case studies illustrate the tangible benefits of effective risk management. They show how proactive risk management can prevent financial losses, protect assets, ensure compliance, and maintain a company's reputation. Seeing these positive outcomes reinforces the importance of investing in robust risk management practices.

For beginners, risk management can seem overwhelming. Case studies break down complex scenarios into manageable pieces, making the subject more approachable. By understanding how other organizations successfully navigated risks, you gain confidence in your ability to do the same.

Each case study typically follows a structured format, detailing the background, risk identification, analysis, response, and outcomes. This provides a clear roadmap of the risk management process, helping you visualize each step and understand how they interconnect. It also highlights the importance of continuous monitoring and adaptation.

By exploring a variety of case studies, you encounter diverse approaches to risk management. This exposure encourages innovative thinking, as you learn to combine different strategies and tailor them to your unique circumstances. It inspires you to think creatively and develop customized solutions to address specific risks. Incorporating lessons from case studies into your decision-making process enhances the quality of your choices. When faced with a risk, you can draw on the experiences of others to guide your actions, ensuring that your decisions are informed and well-considered. Case studies serve as effective communication tools within organizations. They help convey the importance of risk management to stakeholders, demonstrating the potential consequences of unmanaged risks and the benefits of proactive strategies. This understanding fosters a risk-aware culture and encourages collaboration across departments.

Risk management is a dynamic field, constantly evolving in response to new challenges and opportunities. Case studies reflect these changes, providing up-to-date examples of how organizations are adapting to emerging risks. Staying informed about the latest trends and practices ensures that your risk management approach remains relevant and effective.

Case Study 1: Global Bank Corp. (New York, USA)

Scenario: During the transition to a hybrid work model, Global Bank Corp. faced increased cybersecurity threats. Remote work environments made the organization more vulnerable to cyberattacks, with employees accessing sensitive financial data from various locations and networks. The risk management team recognized the urgency of addressing these vulnerabilities to protect customer information and maintain trust.

To combat this, the team implemented a robust cybersecurity framework. They began by conducting a comprehensive risk assessment to identify potential threats and vulnerabilities within the system. Advanced threat detection and response tools, such as SIEM (Security Information and Event Management) systems and endpoint detection and response (EDR) solutions, were integrated into their IT infrastructure. These tools provided real-time monitoring and automated threat responses, significantly enhancing their ability to detect and mitigate cyber threats swiftly. Moreover, the team understood that technology alone wasn't enough. They initiated regular training sessions to educate employees on cybersecurity best practices. These sessions covered topics like recognizing phishing emails, securing home networks, and adhering to data protection policies. The goal was to create a security-conscious culture among all staff members, ensuring that everyone played a role in safeguarding the organization's assets.

Outcome: The proactive approach led to a significant reduction in security incidents. Within a year, the bank reported a 40% decrease in attempted cyberattacks. The continuous training also resulted in employees being more vigilant and responsive to potential threats. Overall, Global Bank Corp. enhanced its resilience against cyber threats, maintaining the integrity and security of its financial operations.

Case Study 2: Tech Innovators Inc. (San Francisco, USA)

Scenario: Tech Innovators Inc., a leading tech company specializing in consumer electronics, faced severe supply chain disruptions during the pandemic. With manufacturing facilities and suppliers spread across the globe, lockdowns and travel restrictions severely impacted their ability to source critical components, threatening production schedules and revenue targets.

To address these challenges, the risk management team adopted an agile risk management framework. This framework emphasized flexibility and rapid response to emerging risks. The team conducted a thorough risk assessment to map out the entire supply chain, identifying key vulnerabilities and potential points of failure. They quickly realized the need to diversify their supplier base to mitigate the risk of over-reliance on a single source. They established partnerships with multiple suppliers across different regions, ensuring that production could continue even if one supplier faced disruptions. Additionally, they implemented real-time monitoring tools to track supply chain status and performance. These tools provided early warnings of potential delays or issues, allowing the team to take preemptive action.

Outcome: The implementation of agile risk management practices paid off significantly. Despite the ongoing global challenges, Tech Innovators Inc. maintained its production schedules and avoided major disruptions. The company reported a 25% increase in supply chain efficiency and a notable improvement in supplier performance metrics. This proactive strategy not only safeguarded their operations but also reinforced their reputation as a resilient and dependable technology provider.

Case Study 3: Secure Finance Ltd. (London, UK)

Scenario: Secure Finance Ltd., a mid-sized financial institution, encountered operational risks due to the sudden shift to remote work. The primary concern was the continuity of critical financial services and maintaining compliance with regulatory requirements.

The risk management team chose to implement the ISO 31000 risk management framework. This framework provided a structured approach to managing risks, emphasizing a systematic process for identifying, assessing, and mitigating risks. The team started by conducting a detailed risk assessment to identify operational risks related to remote work, such as data privacy issues, compliance challenges, and potential disruptions to customer services.

They developed a comprehensive risk management plan, which included enhancing IT infrastructure to support remote operations, implementing secure communication channels, and ensuring all remote activities complied with financial regulations. Regular audits and compliance checks were integrated into their processes to maintain adherence to standards.

Outcome: Secure Finance Ltd. successfully navigated the transition to remote work without any major operational disruptions. Compliance audits showed a high level of adherence to regulatory requirements, and customer service metrics remained stable. The structured approach of the ISO

31000 framework provided a clear roadmap for managing risks, ensuring business continuity and regulatory compliance.

Case Study 4: Global Tech Solutions (Bangalore, India)

Scenario: Global Tech Solutions, a multinational IT services company, faced project delivery risks due to the pandemic. With teams working remotely across different time zones, coordinating project activities and meeting deadlines became challenging.

The risk management team implemented the COSO ERM framework to address these issues. COSO ERM focuses on integrating risk management into the strategic planning and operational processes of the organization. The team conducted a risk assessment to identify key project delivery risks, such as communication breakdowns, resource constraints, and timeline slippages.

They established robust communication protocols and leveraged collaborative tools like Microsoft Teams and Asana to facilitate real-time communication and project tracking. Regular virtual meetings were scheduled to ensure alignment among team members and stakeholders. Additionally, contingency plans were developed to address potential resource shortages or unexpected delays.

Outcome: The use of the COSO ERM framework enabled Global Tech Solutions to enhance project coordination and delivery. Project timelines were met more consistently, and stakeholder satisfaction improved due to the transparent communication and proactive risk management. The company reported a 30% increase in on-time project deliveries, showcasing the effectiveness of the COSO ERM framework in a remote work setting.

Case Study 5: Premier Bank (Sydney, Australia)

Scenario: Premier Bank, a regional bank with a strong customer base, faced reputational risks due to the increasing number of customer complaints about service quality during the pandemic. The bank's transition to a hybrid work model had affected its customer service operations.

The risk management team adopted the NIST Cybersecurity Framework to strengthen their cybersecurity posture and address service quality issues. They began by identifying the root causes of the complaints, which included slow response times and inadequate security measures for online banking services. The team enhanced their cybersecurity measures by implementing multi-factor authentication (MFA), encrypted communication channels, and regular security updates. They also trained customer service representatives on handling common issues and cybersecurity best practices to ensure a seamless customer experience.

Outcome: The implementation of the NIST Cybersecurity Framework resulted in a significant improvement in service quality and customer satisfaction. The number of complaints decreased by 40%, and customer feedback highlighted the enhanced security measures. Premier Bank's proactive risk management approach helped restore customer trust and maintain its reputation in the market.

Chapter 6:

FRAMEWORK FOUNDATIONS

"Do not be embarrassed by your failures, learn from them and start again."

— *Richard Branson*

Handling Real-Time Crises

The ability to respond quickly and effectively to crises is critical for any organization. Risk managers are essential in guiding organizations through these tough situations, helping them manage unexpected events and come out stronger. Here, we'll explore how to handle real-time crises using the example of a sudden product recall.

Dealing with a Product Recall

Imagine it's a regular Wednesday morning. You're checking the latest risk reports when suddenly, an alert pops up on your screen—a major flaw has been discovered in one of your company's products. The product poses a safety risk, and you need to recall it immediately. Every second counts, and you need to act fast.

Step 1: Activate the Immediate Response Steps

1. **Contain the Issue:** The first step is to stop the product from being sold. Contact all distributors and retailers to halt sales and remove the product from shelves.
2. **Assess the Impact:** Quickly figure out the extent of the issue. Determine how many products are affected, where they are located, and the potential risk to consumers.
3. **Activate the Crisis Management Team:** Inform the crisis management team immediately. This group is trained to

handle such situations and will take charge of managing the recall.

4. **Communicate with Stakeholders:** During a crisis, being transparent is crucial. Inform senior management, legal teams, and regulatory bodies if necessary. Keep customers updated about the recall and what is being done to address the issue.

Case Study: Toyota's Accelerator Pedal Recall

Background: In 2009-2010, Toyota faced a significant crisis when reports emerged of unintended acceleration in some of its vehicles. This issue was linked to faulty accelerator pedals that could become stuck or return slowly to idle, posing serious safety risks.

Immediate Response Steps by Toyota -

Contain the Issue: Upon identifying the problem, Toyota quickly issued a recall for millions of vehicles worldwide. They instructed dealerships to stop selling affected models and began the process of notifying owners.

Assess the Impact: Toyota conducted an in-depth analysis to determine the scope of the issue. They identified which models were affected and the potential risks involved. This included checking how many vehicles were on the road and the geographical spread of the problem.

Activate the Crisis Management Team: Toyota's crisis management team, including engineers, safety experts, and communications professionals, worked around the clock to address the issue. They coordinated efforts to understand the root cause and develop a solution.

Communicate with Stakeholders: Transparency was key in managing the crisis. Toyota issued public statements, held press conferences, and communicated directly with customers through various channels. They explained the problem, the steps being taken to fix it, and how customers could stay safe.

Implement Solutions: Toyota developed a fix for the accelerator pedals and began repairing affected vehicles. They also enhanced their quality control processes to prevent future issues.

Monitor and Review: After the initial response, Toyota continued to monitor the situation, ensuring that all recalled vehicles were repaired and addressing any new issues that arose. They also reviewed their crisis management strategies to improve their response to future incidents.

Outcome: Although the recall was costly and temporarily damaged Toyota's reputation, the company's swift and comprehensive response helped restore customer trust. Toyota's commitment to transparency and safety reassured customers and stakeholders, demonstrating the importance of effective crisis management.

Lessons Learned

- **Speed and Efficiency:** Acting quickly to contain and address the issue is crucial in a crisis.
- **Clear Communication:** Keeping stakeholders informed with transparent and honest communication helps maintain trust.
- **Preparedness:** Having a well-prepared crisis management team and plan in place is essential for handling unexpected events.
- **Continuous Improvement:** Learning from the crisis and improving processes helps prevent future issues.

Step 2: Communicate with Stakeholders

Clear and timely communication is crucial during a crisis. It's important to inform all relevant stakeholders, including employees, customers, and regulatory bodies. Being transparent helps maintain trust and credibility.

Develop a Communication Plan

First, you need to create a communication plan. This plan should outline how you'll inform different groups. For employees, you need to provide clear instructions on handling customer inquiries. Customers should be informed about the issue and advised on what steps they should take. Regulatory bodies need to be notified to comply with legal requirements.

Case Study: Johnson & Johnson's Tylenol Crisis

Background: In 1982, Johnson & Johnson faced a severe crisis when several people died after taking Tylenol capsules that had been laced with cyanide. The company's swift and transparent communication played a crucial role in managing the situation effectively.

How did Johnson & Johnson handle the crisis?

Immediate Action: As soon as Johnson & Johnson learned about the tampering, they immediately alerted the public and stopped the production and advertising of Tylenol. They also issued a nationwide recall of Tylenol products, pulling 31 million bottles from the shelves.

Transparency: The company managed to communicate openly with the media and the public about what had happened and what steps they were taking to address the issue. They held regular press conferences and provided updates on the situation.

Customer Safety: Johnson & Johnson set up a hotline for consumers to call with concerns and provided frequent updates through the media. They also offered to exchange all Tylenol capsules already purchased for tablets, which were safer.

Regulatory Compliance: They worked closely with regulatory bodies to ensure all safety standards were met and to develop new tamper-resistant packaging, which became an industry standard.

Outcome: Despite the crisis, Johnson & Johnson's handling of the situation helped them regain public trust. Their commitment to customer safety and transparent communication were key factors in their recovery. The company's market share, which had plummeted during the crisis, rebounded within a year.

Lessons Learned:

From Johnson & Johnson's Tylenol crisis, we learn the importance of:

- **Immediate Action:** Quickly addressing the issue shows that the company is taking the problem seriously.
- **Transparency:** Being open and honest with the public helps maintain trust.
- **Customer Focus:** Prioritizing customer safety and providing clear guidance helps mitigate panic and confusion.
- **Regulatory Compliance:** Working closely with regulatory

bodies ensures all actions meet legal requirements and helps restore credibility.

Step 3: Mitigate the Impact

Once the incident response plan is activated and stakeholders are informed, the next step is to mitigate the impact of the crisis. This involves working closely with relevant teams to contain the issue and prevent further damage.

Coordinating Efforts

You need to oversee efforts to isolate the affected areas, fix vulnerabilities, and enhance safety measures. Additionally, you should work with legal and compliance teams to ensure that all actions comply with regulatory requirements and minimize legal risks.

Case Study: SolarWinds Cyberattack

Background: In 2020, the SolarWinds cyberattack compromised numerous organizations, including Fortune 500 companies and government agencies. These organizations had to act quickly to contain the breach and mitigate its impact.

This is how SolarWinds handle the attack:

Isolation of Affected Systems: Companies identified and isolated the compromised systems to prevent the attackers from causing further harm. This step was crucial in stopping the spread of the breach.

Patch Vulnerabilities: Security teams worked tirelessly to identify and patch the vulnerabilities that the attackers exploited. This included updating software and implementing new security measures.

Enhancing Security Protocols: Organizations reviewed and strengthened their security protocols to prevent future attacks. This involved updating firewalls, enhancing monitoring systems, and increasing security awareness among employees.

Collaboration with Experts: Many companies hired external cybersecurity firms to conduct forensic investigations. These experts helped identify the full extent of the breach, ensuring that no hidden threats remained.

Legal and Compliance Coordination: Legal teams ensured that all actions taken were in compliance with regulations. This helped minimize potential legal repercussions and protected the organizations from further liability.

Outcome: By taking these steps, the affected organizations were able to contain the breach and start rebuilding their defenses. The collaboration between internal teams and external experts was vital in mitigating the impact and enhancing future security measures.

Lessons Learned:

From the response to the SolarWinds cyberattack, we learn the importance of:

- **Immediate Isolation:** Quickly isolating affected systems to prevent further damage.
- **Rapid Patch Deployment:** Identifying and fixing vulnerabilities as soon as possible.
- **Security Protocol Enhancement:** Continuously improving security measures to stay ahead of potential threats.
- **Expert Collaboration:** Bringing in external experts for thorough investigations and solutions.
- **Regulatory Compliance:** Ensuring all actions comply with legal requirements to avoid additional issues.

Step 4: Review and Learn

After the immediate crisis is managed and the situation is stable, it's essential to conduct a detailed post-incident review. This step is crucial for understanding what happened, learning from the experience, and making improvements to be better prepared for future incidents.

Conducting the Post-Incident Review

1. **Gather Your Team:** Bring together everyone who was involved in managing the crisis, including members from

different departments such as IT, security, legal, communications, and any other relevant areas. This helps ensure a comprehensive review from multiple perspectives.

2. **Thorough Analysis:** Conduct a detailed analysis of the incident. This involves looking at the sequence of events, identifying the root causes, and assessing the effectiveness of the response. Key areas to examine include:

    a. **Detection and Response:** How quickly was the incident detected? Were the initial responses effective?

    b. **Communication:** Were stakeholders informed promptly and adequately? Was the communication clear and effective?

    c. **Coordination:** How well did different teams work together? Were there any coordination issues?

    d. **Containment and Mitigation:** How effective were the efforts to contain and mitigate the impact of the incident?

3. **Evaluate What Worked Well:** Identify the aspects of the response that were successful. This could include timely detection, effective communication, strong teamwork, or successful containment strategies. Recognizing these strengths helps reinforce good practices.

4. **Identify Areas for Improvement:** Pinpoint areas where the response could have been better. This might involve delays in detection, communication breakdowns, lack of resources,

or inadequate procedures. Understanding these weaknesses is critical for future improvement.

Documenting Findings

- **Create a Detailed Report:** Document all the findings from the post-incident review in a detailed report. This report should include:
  - A timeline of the incident and response actions
  - Key successes and strengths
  - Identified weaknesses and areas for improvement
  - Recommendations for changes and enhancements
- **Update the Incident Response Plan:** Based on the findings, update your incident response plan. This might involve revising procedures, adding new steps, or clarifying roles and responsibilities. Ensure that the updated plan addresses the identified weaknesses and incorporates the lessons learned.

Implementing Changes

- **Enhance Training and Awareness:** Provide additional training to employees based on the lessons learned. This could include new protocols, improved communication strategies, or specific technical training to address identified gaps.
- **Improve Tools and Resources:** Upgrade or acquire new

tools and resources that can help in better managing future incidents. This might include enhanced detection systems, improved communication platforms, or additional personnel.

- **Conduct Regular Drills:** Regularly practice the updated incident response plan through drills and simulations. This helps ensure that everyone is familiar with the new procedures and can respond effectively in real situations.

Continuous Improvement

- **Regular Reviews:** Conduct regular reviews of your incident response plan, even when no incidents occur. This helps ensure that the plan remains up-to-date and effective in the face of evolving threats.
- **Feedback Loop:** Establish a feedback loop where team members can continuously provide input on the incident response plan and suggest improvements. This helps maintain a culture of continuous improvement and adaptability.

Chapter 7

LEARNING FROM THE PAST

"The only way to eliminate risk is to eliminate uncertainty."

— *Ken Fisher*

Leveraging Technology in Risk Management

In today's rapidly evolving world, technology has become a cornerstone of effective risk management, particularly in hybrid work environments where the dynamics of collaboration and security are constantly shifting. Let's dive into the critical role that various technologies play in identifying, assessing, and mitigating risks, and explore how they can be harnessed to build a resilient organization.

AI and Machine Learning: The Predictive Powerhouses

Artificial Intelligence (AI) and Machine Learning (ML) have revolutionized the field of risk management by offering predictive analytics and advanced risk assessment capabilities. These technologies can analyze vast amounts of data to identify patterns and predict potential risks, allowing organizations to take proactive measures.

Consider the case of JP Morgan & Chase, one of the largest banks in the world. They implemented AI-driven models to analyze transaction data and detect fraudulent activities in real-time. By training their algorithms on historical data, JP Morgan's AI systems can identify unusual patterns that may indicate fraud, triggering alerts for further investigation. This predictive capability significantly reduces the response time, mitigating the risk of large-scale fraud.

The core principle behind using AI and ML in risk management is their ability to learn from data continuously. These systems improve over time, becoming more accurate in their predictions as they are exposed to new data. However, it's essential to have robust data governance practices in place to ensure the quality and integrity of the data being used.

AI and ML provide unparalleled capabilities in handling complex datasets and identifying risks that may not be evident through traditional analysis. They excel in processing real-time data, which is crucial for timely risk mitigation. However, their effectiveness is highly dependent on the quality of the data and the algorithms used. There's also a need for continuous monitoring and updating of these systems to adapt to new threats and changing environments.

Data Analytics: Uncovering Hidden Insights

Data analytics is another powerful tool in the risk management arsenal. By analyzing large volumes of data, risk managers can uncover patterns and trends that provide insights into emerging risks. This data-driven approach allows for more informed decision-making and the development of targeted mitigation strategies.

Walmart, the retail giant, employs data analytics extensively to manage risks across its supply chain. By analyzing data from various sources—such as sales figures, supplier performance, and market trends—Walmart can identify potential supply chain disruptions before they occur. For instance, if data shows a supplier consistently delays shipments, Walmart can proactively seek alternative suppliers to ensure continuous product availability.

Data analytics also plays a crucial role in customer risk management. For example, insurance companies like Allstate use data analytics to assess risk profiles of their customers. By analyzing data on driving habits, accident history, and even social media activity, Allstate can more accurately price their insurance policies and reduce the risk of underwriting losses.

The strength of data analytics lies in its ability to process and make sense of vast amounts of data, providing actionable insights. It enables organizations to move from reactive to proactive risk management. However, data analytics requires significant investment in technology and skilled personnel. Additionally, ensuring data privacy and security is paramount, as mishandling sensitive data can lead to compliance issues and reputational damage.

Collaboration Platforms: Bridging the Communication Gap

In a hybrid work environment, maintaining effective communication and collaboration is vital for risk management. Collaboration platforms like Slack, Microsoft Teams, and Asana play a critical role in keeping remote and in-office teams aligned and informed.

Slack, for example, is widely used across industries to facilitate real-time communication. During the COVID-19 pandemic, many companies, such as Airbnb, relied heavily on Slack to coordinate their risk management efforts. With team members scattered across the globe, Slack allowed Airbnb to maintain seamless communication, share important updates instantly, and collaborate on risk mitigation strategies effectively.

Microsoft Teams is another robust platform that integrates various tools needed for collaboration. Unilever, a global consumer goods company, uses Microsoft Teams to connect its diverse workforce. This platform allows Unilever to host virtual meetings, share documents securely, and manage projects collaboratively, ensuring that all stakeholders are on the same page regarding risk management.

Collaboration platforms enhance communication and coordination, which are essential for timely risk management. They offer flexibility, enabling teams to work together regardless of their physical location. However, over-reliance on these platforms can lead to challenges such as information overload and potential security vulnerabilities. It's crucial to establish clear communication protocols and security measures to mitigate these risks.

Cybersecurity Tools: Fortifying the Digital Fortress

In the age of digital transformation, cybersecurity is a top priority for organizations. Implementing advanced threat detection and response tools is essential for protecting against cyber threats and ensuring the integrity of critical data.

IBM uses a multi-layered cybersecurity approach to protect its vast digital infrastructure. They employ IBM QRadar, a security information and event management (SIEM) system, which collects and analyzes data from various sources to detect potential security threats. When an anomaly is detected, QRadar triggers alerts, allowing the security team to respond swiftly.

Pharmaceutical giant Pfizer also leverages cybersecurity tools to safeguard its sensitive research and development data. Pfizer uses endpoint protection platforms that monitor and secure devices connected to the network, ensuring that any suspicious activity is immediately flagged and addressed. This proactive approach is crucial in an industry where data breaches can have catastrophic consequences.

Cybersecurity tools provide robust protection against a wide range of threats, from malware to advanced persistent threats. They enable real-time threat detection and response, minimizing the potential damage from cyber attacks. However, these tools require continuous updating and monitoring to stay effective against evolving threats. Moreover, cybersecurity is not solely about technology; it also involves educating employees about best practices and maintaining a culture of security awareness.

Use-Cases:

The successful implementation of these technologies can be seen across various industries, showcasing their transformative impact on risk management.

1. Financial Sector: Global Bank Corp.:

Scenario: Global Bank Corp., headquartered in New York, encountered heightened cybersecurity risks during its shift to a hybrid work model. To address these challenges, the risk management team implemented a robust cybersecurity framework integrating advanced threat detection and response tools. They also conducted regular training sessions to ensure all employees were well-versed in cybersecurity best practices.

Outcome: This proactive approach resulted in a notable decrease in security incidents and bolstered the bank's overall resilience against cyber threats. By harnessing AI and machine learning capabilities, the bank was able to anticipate and mitigate potential threats proactively.

2. Technology Sector: Tech Innovators Inc.

Scenario: Tech Innovators Inc., headquartered in San

Francisco, faced significant supply chain disruptions during the pandemic. In response, the risk management team adopted an agile risk management framework, enabling swift identification and mitigation of supply chain risks. They diversified their supplier base and deployed real-time monitoring tools.

Outcome: As a result of these proactive measures, the company successfully maintained its production schedules and mitigated the impact of supply chain disruptions. Leveraging advanced data analytics, Tech Innovators Inc. was able to anticipate potential disruptions and adapt their strategies effectively.

3. Retail Sector: Walmart

Scenario: Walmart, headquartered in Bentonville, Arkansas, needed to manage risks across its vast supply chain effectively. By analyzing data from various sources, Walmart could identify potential supply chain disruptions and take proactive measures.

Outcome: Walmart's proactive risk management approach ensured continuous product availability, even during peak seasons and unexpected disruptions. Data analytics allowed Walmart to make informed decisions and maintain a resilient supply chain.

4. Hospitality Sector: Marriott International

Scenario: Marriott International, based in Bethesda, Maryland, faced a significant data breach affecting millions of guests. The company needed to manage the crisis and communicate effectively with all stakeholders.

Outcome: Marriott's transparent and timely communication efforts helped maintain customer trust and manage the breach's fallout effectively. The use of collaboration platforms ensured that all teams were aligned and could respond promptly.

5. Healthcare Sector: Pfizer

Scenario: Pfizer, headquartered in New York, needed to protect its sensitive research and development data from cyber threats. The company implemented advanced cybersecurity tools and conducted regular training sessions for employees.

Outcome: Pfizer's robust cybersecurity measures safeguarded critical data and ensured the integrity of their research processes. The proactive approach minimized the risk of data breaches and protected Pfizer's intellectual property.

Conclusion

Technology has become an indispensable ally in the realm of risk management, especially in the hybrid work era. By harnessing the power of AI and machine learning for predictive analytics, leveraging data analytics to uncover hidden insights, utilizing collaboration platforms to maintain seamless communication, and employing advanced cybersecurity tools to protect against digital threats, organizations can significantly enhance their risk management capabilities.

The examples of Global Bank Corp., Tech Innovators Inc., Walmart, Marriott International, and Pfizer illustrate the transformative impact of these technologies. Each company leveraged specific tools and frameworks to address their unique challenges, demonstrating the versatility and effectiveness of technology in risk management.

As we move forward, the integration of technology into risk management practices will continue to evolve, driven by advancements in AI, data analytics, and cybersecurity. By staying ahead of the curve and embracing these innovations, organizations can navigate the complexities of modern risk landscapes with confidence and resilience.

Chapter 8

CRISIS COMMAND

Creating a culture that prioritizes risk management is crucial for any organization aiming for long-term success and resilience. In this chapter, we'll explore how to build such a culture, emphasizing the importance of training programs, leadership commitment, open communication, and continuous improvement. By integrating these elements, organizations can proactively manage risks and adapt to evolving challenges.

Training Programs: Empowering Employees with Knowledge

In addition to being the foundation of a risk-aware culture, training programs equip employees with the knowledge and skills necessary to identify, assess, and mitigate risks. Regular training sessions ensure that everyone understands their role in the organization's risk management strategy.

Consider the example of "Delta Airlines". Delta conducts comprehensive training programs for all employees, from pilots to ground staff, emphasizing safety and risk management. These programs include simulations of emergency scenarios, teaching staff how to respond swiftly and effectively. Delta also uses data analytics to identify areas where additional training is needed, ensuring that their workforce is always prepared for potential risks.

To implement effective training programs, organizations

can utilize a variety of tools and frameworks. For instance, the **Enterprise Risk Management (ERM) framework** provides a structured approach to identifying and managing risks across an organization. Training sessions can be designed around ERM principles, helping employees understand how to apply these concepts in their daily work. Additionally, e-learning platforms like "Coursera", "Udemy" or "LinkedIn Learning" offer courses on risk management, providing flexible training options that can be tailored to specific organizational needs.

The strength of regular training programs lies in their ability to keep the workforce informed and prepared. They foster a sense of ownership and responsibility towards risk management. However, one limitation is the potential for training fatigue. Employees may become disengaged if training sessions are too frequent or repetitive. To mitigate this, organizations should ensure that training content is engaging, relevant, and updated regularly.

Leadership Commitment: Setting the Tone from the Top

Leadership commitment is vital for embedding a risk-aware culture within an organization. When leaders prioritize risk management and model risk-aware behaviors, it sends a powerful message to employees about the importance of these practices.

HSBC, one of the world's largest banking and financial services organizations, exemplifies strong leadership commitment to risk management. The bank's leadership team regularly communicates the importance of risk management through town halls, internal communications, and dedicated risk management meetings. They have established a Risk Committee at the board level, which oversees the bank's risk management framework and ensures that adequate resources are allocated to risk management initiatives. Leaders can also use procurement strategies to support risk management efforts. For example, investing in advanced risk management software like **RiskWatch** or **MetricStream** demonstrates a commitment to equipping the organization with the tools needed to manage risks effectively. These tools provide comprehensive risk assessment and reporting capabilities, helping leaders make informed decisions.

Leadership commitment drives a top-down approach to risk management, ensuring that it is integrated into the organization's strategic objectives. It fosters a culture of accountability and continuous improvement. However, the limitation is that if leaders do not consistently demonstrate their commitment, it can undermine the organization's risk management efforts. Leaders must remain actively engaged and transparent in their risk management practices to maintain credibility.

Open Communication: Encouraging Transparency and Reporting

Open communication is essential for a risk-aware culture. Employees should feel comfortable reporting risks and near-misses without fear of retribution. Creating a safe environment for raising concerns enables organizations to identify and address potential issues before they escalate.

At **Toyota**, open communication is a core component of their risk management strategy. The company has implemented a "Stop and Fix" policy, empowering employees to halt production if they identify a safety issue. This policy encourages immediate reporting and resolution of risks, preventing small issues from becoming major problems. Toyota also conducts regular risk assessments and encourages employees to participate in risk identification processes.

To facilitate open communication, organizations can use collaboration platforms like "Slack" or "Microsoft Teams". These tools provide channels for reporting risks and sharing information across teams. Additionally, anonymous reporting systems can be implemented to allow employees to report concerns without fear of reprisal.

The strength of open communication lies in its ability to surface risks early and promote a proactive approach to risk management. It builds trust and fosters a collaborative culture.

However, the limitation is that without proper mechanisms to address reported risks, employees may become disillusioned. Organizations must ensure that reported risks are taken seriously and addressed promptly to maintain trust.

Continuous Improvement: Adapting and Evolving

Continuous improvement is the cornerstone of a risk-aware culture. Risk management practices should be regularly reviewed and updated based on feedback and lessons learned. This iterative approach ensures that the organization remains resilient and can adapt to new challenges. **Google** is renowned for its culture of continuous improvement. The company conducts regular post-incident reviews, known as "blameless postmortems," to analyze what went wrong during a crisis and how it can be prevented in the future. These reviews focus on identifying systemic issues rather than assigning blame, fostering a culture of learning and improvement. Google also uses data analytics to monitor risks and track the effectiveness of mitigation strategies, ensuring that their risk management practices evolve with changing circumstances. To support continuous improvement, organizations can implement frameworks like **ISO 31000**, which provides guidelines for risk management. Regular audits and assessments can help identify areas for improvement and ensure that risk management practices align with industry standards. Additionally, feedback mechanisms, such as surveys and suggestion boxes, can provide valuable insights from employees on how to enhance risk management processes.

Continuous improvement ensures that risk management practices remain effective and relevant. It builds a culture of innovation and adaptability. However, the limitation is that it requires a commitment to ongoing evaluation and adjustment, which can be resource-intensive. Organizations must balance the need for continuous improvement with operational constraints to maintain effectiveness.

Real-World Applications and Outcomes

The integration of these elements—training programs, leadership commitment, open communication, and continuous improvement—into a cohesive risk management strategy can significantly enhance an organization's ability to manage risks.

Case Study: Delta Airlines

Delta Airlines, headquartered in Atlanta, Georgia, is a prime example of a company that has effectively integrated a risk-aware culture through comprehensive training programs. For a beginner, understanding how Delta managed risks begins with recognizing the aviation industry's inherent complexities and potential hazards.

Scenario: Aviation involves numerous risks, from mechanical failures to weather-related disruptions and security threats.

Given the high stakes, Delta Airlines prioritizes risk management to ensure passenger safety and operational continuity. They faced a significant challenge in maintaining consistent risk management practices across a diverse and global workforce, including pilots, cabin crew, maintenance teams, and ground staff.

Risk Management Strategy:

Delta implemented a multi-faceted training program aimed at empowering all employees with the necessary skills and knowledge to manage risks. This program includes:

- **Comprehensive Training Programs:** Delta conducts rigorous training sessions for its employees. For pilots, this involves simulators that replicate various emergency scenarios, such as engine failures or severe weather conditions. Ground staff and maintenance teams undergo regular safety drills and technical training to handle equipment and operational risks.
- **Data-Driven Approach:** Delta uses data analytics to monitor and assess risks continuously. By analyzing data from past incidents, they identify trends and areas needing improvement. This proactive approach helps in updating training programs to address emerging risks.
- **Cross-Functional Training:** Recognizing that risk management is a collective responsibility, Delta offers

cross-functional training. This means that pilots, cabin crew, and ground staff all understand each other's roles and how they can collectively manage risks. This holistic understanding fosters better teamwork and communication during crises.

Outcome: Delta's comprehensive risk management strategy has led to a significant reduction in safety incidents. By regularly updating their training programs based on data insights, they ensure that all employees are well-prepared to handle emergencies. This proactive and inclusive approach has helped Delta maintain a strong safety record and instill a culture of risk awareness across the organization.

Case Study 2: Amazon

Amazon, the global e-commerce giant headquartered in Seattle, Washington, demonstrates how effective communication and leadership commitment are crucial in building a risk-aware culture.

Scenario: Amazon's extensive operations include a vast network of warehouses, delivery systems, and a diverse workforce spread across different countries. Managing risks in such a complex environment is challenging, especially considering the high demand for efficiency and customer satisfaction. One notable risk scenario involved operational disruptions during the peak holiday season, where any failure in the supply chain could lead to significant losses.

Risk Management Strategy

Amazon's approach to managing risks involves several key strategies:

- **Regular Updates and Transparent Communication:** Amazon ensures that all employees and stakeholders are informed about potential risks and ongoing risk management activities. They hold regular meetings and use internal communication platforms to disseminate critical information.
- **Cultural Sensitivity and Inclusion:** Understanding the diverse backgrounds of its workforce, Amazon tailors its risk communication strategies to accommodate cultural differences. This includes multilingual training materials and culturally sensitive risk management protocols.
- **Leadership Commitment:** Amazon's leadership plays an active role in risk management. Senior leaders regularly participate in risk assessment meetings and model risk-aware behavior. This top-down approach ensures that risk management is a priority at all organizational levels.

Outcome: Amazon's integrated approach has enabled them to manage risks effectively, even during peak operational periods. The combination of regular updates, cultural sensitivity, strong leadership commitment, and advanced technology has created a resilient and adaptable risk management culture. As a result, Amazon continues to maintain its operational efficiency and customer satisfaction, even in the face of potential disruptions.

Case Study 3: Toyota

Toyota, a leading automotive manufacturer based in Toyota City, Japan, offers an example of how continuous improvement and employee engagement are vital for effective risk management.

Scenario: Toyota's production system is renowned for its efficiency and quality, but it also faces risks related to supply chain disruptions and production line issues. In the past, Toyota encountered significant challenges due to natural disasters affecting its suppliers and production facilities.

Risk Management Strategy

Toyota's risk management strategy focuses on continuous improvement (Kaizen) and employee involvement:

- **Kaizen (Continuous Improvement):** Toyota's commitment to continuous improvement involves regularly assessing and refining their processes. Employees at all levels are encouraged to suggest improvements and report potential risks. This bottom-up approach ensures that risks are identified and mitigated promptly.
- **Employee Training and Engagement:** Toyota conducts ongoing training sessions for employees, emphasizing the

importance of quality control and risk management. Workers are trained to identify issues on the production line and take immediate action to prevent defects.

- **Supplier Risk Management:** Toyota works closely with its suppliers to manage risks. They conduct regular audits and collaborate with suppliers to develop contingency plans for potential disruptions. This proactive approach ensures that supply chain risks are minimized.
- **Advanced Monitoring Tools:** Toyota uses advanced monitoring tools to track production processes and identify potential risks. Real-time data analytics help in predicting and mitigating issues before they escalate.

Outcome: Toyota's focus on continuous improvement and employee engagement has resulted in a robust risk management culture. Their proactive strategies have enabled them to recover quickly from disruptions and maintain high standards of quality and efficiency. By fostering a culture where every employee is a risk manager, Toyota has built a resilient and adaptive organization.

To summarize, building a risk-aware culture is not just a strategic initiative; it's a fundamental shift in how an organization operates and perceives challenges. The examples of Delta Airlines, Amazon, and Toyota demonstrate the diverse approaches companies can take to foster such a culture, highlighting the importance of comprehensive training programs, leadership commitment, open communication, and continuous improvement.

At Delta Airlines, the emphasis on rigorous and data-driven training programs ensured that all employees were well-prepared to manage risks, leading to enhanced safety and operational efficiency. Amazon's strategy of leveraging technology and maintaining transparent communication underscores the need for adaptability and cultural sensitivity in a globalized workforce. Toyota's Kaizen approach, with its focus on continuous improvement and employee engagement, illustrates how a proactive and inclusive risk management strategy can lead to long-term resilience and operational excellence.

By integrating these principles, organizations can create an environment where risk management is everyone's responsibility. Training programs should not only impart knowledge but also instill a mindset that prioritizes risk awareness. Leadership must actively support and participate in risk management initiatives, setting a precedent for the entire organization. Open communication channels encourage employees to report risks without fear, fostering a culture of transparency and trust. Lastly, continuous improvement ensures that risk management practices evolve with the changing landscape, keeping the organization agile and prepared for future challenges.

In conclusion, a risk-aware culture is a vital component of a successful and resilient organization. By adopting these strategies and learning from the examples of leading companies, organizations can enhance their ability to manage risks proactively, ensuring long-term success and sustainability in an ever-changing business environment.

Chapter 9

TECH-ENABLED RISK MASTERY

"In times of change, learners inherit the earth, while the learned find themselves beautifully equipped to deal with a world that no longer exists."

— *Eric Hoffer*

The landscape of risk management is constantly evolving. As organizations navigate the complexities of a hybrid work environment, they must also prepare for future uncertainties. This chapter explores the emerging trends in risk management and how organizations can adapt to these changes to remain resilient and competitive.

Increased Reliance on Technology:

Artificial Intelligence (AI) and Machine Learning (ML) are powerful tools transforming the field of risk management. These technologies allow companies to move beyond reactive measures and adopt a predictive, proactive approach. AI and ML are particularly effective because they can process vast amounts of data from multiple sources, identify patterns, and predict potential risks. This capability is crucial in a globalized economy where businesses face a multitude of risks, ranging from financial fraud to supply chain disruptions.

How AI and ML Work in Risk Management?

To understand how AI and ML can be used in risk management, let's break down their functionalities and applications in simple terms:

1. **Data Processing and Analysis:** AI systems can handle enormous datasets much faster and more accurately than humans. For example, a multinational company might

collect data from financial transactions, market trends, social media, and news articles. An AI system can analyze all this data to identify unusual patterns or anomalies that might indicate a risk.

2. **Pattern Recognition:** One of the key strengths of AI is its ability to recognize patterns in data. For instance, in the financial sector, AI can detect unusual activity in bank accounts that might signal fraudulent transactions. These patterns can be extremely complex and subtle, often beyond the capability of human analysts to detect.

3. **Predictive Capabilities:** Machine Learning, a subset of AI, excels at predicting future events based on historical data. It learns from past data, continually improving its predictions as it is exposed to new data. This means that over time, an ML system becomes better at forecasting risks.

To illustrate how AI and ML are used in practice, let's consider the example of Amazon, a global e-commerce giant. Amazon operates an extensive supply chain, sourcing products from all over the world and delivering them to customers in a timely manner. Managing such a complex supply chain involves significant risks, including delays due to weather conditions, political instability, or logistical issues.

Amazon uses AI to monitor and manage its supply chain proactively. Here's how:

Data Collection: Amazon collects data from various sources, including weather forecasts, news reports, supplier performance metrics, and even social media trends. This data is fed into their AI systems.

Risk Prediction: The AI system analyzes this data to predict potential disruptions. For example, if a severe storm is forecasted in a region where a key supplier is located, the AI system can anticipate delays.

Proactive Mitigation: Once a potential risk is identified, the AI system can recommend actions to mitigate the impact. In the case of the storm, the system might suggest rerouting shipments through a different supplier or increasing stock levels in affected regions beforehand.

Continuous Learning: The ML component continuously learns from new data, improving its predictive accuracy over time. Each time a disruption occurs and is managed, the system learns from the outcome, refining its future predictions and recommendations.

Global Impact and Adaptability

The use of AI and ML in risk management is not limited to large corporations like Amazon. Businesses of all sizes and across industries can benefit from these technologies.

Here's how companies around the world are leveraging AI and ML:

Financial Institutions: Banks and insurance companies use AI to detect and prevent fraud. For example, AI can analyze transaction patterns and flag suspicious activities for further investigation. This proactive approach helps protect customers and reduce financial losses.

Healthcare: Hospitals use AI to predict patient admission rates and manage resources effectively. During the COVID-19 pandemic, AI helped predict outbreak patterns and optimize supply chains for medical supplies.

Manufacturing: Manufacturers use AI to predict equipment failures and schedule maintenance before breakdowns occur. This minimizes downtime and keeps production lines running smoothly.

While AI and ML offer significant advantages, they also come with challenges. These technologies require large amounts of data and sophisticated algorithms, which can be costly to develop and maintain. Additionally, there are concerns about data privacy and security, especially when handling sensitive information.

However, as technology continues to advance, the barriers to entry are decreasing. Cloud computing and open-source AI tools are making these technologies more accessible to businesses of all sizes. Looking ahead, we can expect AI and ML to become even more integrated into risk management practices, helping organizations around the world anticipate and mitigate risks more effectively.

Big Data and Analytics in Risk Management:

Big Data and Analytics have revolutionized the way organizations manage risks. In simple terms, big data refers to vast amounts of data that are too large or complex for traditional data-processing methods. Data analytics involves examining this data to uncover patterns, trends, and insights. For businesses, this means they can now detect risks earlier and respond more effectively.

Imagine a bank handling millions of transactions every day. Sifting through all that data manually would be impossible. But with big data and analytics, the bank can monitor these transactions in real-time and spot any unusual activity that might indicate fraud. This is just one example of how these technologies are used to improve risk management on a global scale.

How Big Data and Analytics Work in Risk Management?

To understand how big data and analytics are applied in risk management, let's break it down:

Data Collection: Organizations collect data from various sources. This can include transaction records, social media activity, customer feedback, market trends, and more. The sheer volume and variety of data collected can be overwhelming.

Data Processing: Advanced algorithms and data processing tools are used to handle and analyze this data. These tools can sort through the noise to find relevant information and identify patterns that might indicate a risk.

Pattern Recognition: Data analytics tools excel at recognizing patterns and trends within large datasets. For example, if a customer suddenly starts making purchases in different countries within a short period, this could be flagged as suspicious activity.

Predictive Analytics: Beyond just identifying current risks, these tools can also predict future risks based on historical data. By analyzing past events, the system can forecast potential future scenarios and help organizations prepare for them.

One of the most notable examples of using big data and analytics in risk management is JP Morgan & Chase. Here's how they do it:

Transaction Monitoring: JP Morgan & Chase processes millions of transactions daily. Their data analytics system monitors each transaction in real-time, analyzing patterns and looking for anomalies.

Anomaly Detection: The system uses sophisticated algorithms to identify deviations from normal behavior. For instance, if a customer usually makes purchases in New York but suddenly makes several transactions in Europe, this might be flagged as suspicious.

Fraud Prevention: Once an anomaly is detected, the system flags it for further review. This allows the bank to investigate and take swift action if necessary, such as contacting the customer to verify the transactions or temporarily freezing the account to prevent further potential fraud.

Continuous Improvement: JP Morgan & Chase's system continuously learns from new data. Each time a new fraud attempt is detected and stopped, the system updates its algorithms to recognize similar patterns in the future. This means the system becomes more effective over time.

Global Impact and Adaptability

Big data and analytics are not just for large corporations like JP Morgan & Chase. Businesses of all sizes and across various industries can benefit from these technologies. Here's how they are applied globally:

Retail: Retailers use data analytics to monitor purchasing patterns and detect theft or fraud. For example, if a store notices a sudden spike in high-value item purchases that are later returned, this could indicate a fraudulent scheme.

Supply Chain Management: Manufacturers use big data to monitor their supply chains. By analyzing data from suppliers, transportation networks, and inventory levels, they can identify potential disruptions and take preventive measures. For example, if data shows a supplier consistently has delays, the manufacturer might look for alternative suppliers.

While the benefits of big data and analytics are significant, there are also challenges to consider:

Data Privacy and Security: Handling large volumes of data comes with the responsibility of ensuring it is secure and privacy is maintained. Organizations must comply with data protection regulations to avoid legal issues and maintain customer trust.

Data Quality: The insights gained from data analytics are only as good as the data itself. Poor-quality data can lead to incorrect conclusions and ineffective risk management strategies. Therefore, organizations need to invest in systems and processes that ensure data accuracy and integrity.

Cost and Complexity: Implementing big data and analytics systems can be expensive and complex, especially for smaller businesses. However, as technology advances, more affordable and user-friendly solutions are becoming available.

Skill Requirements: Effective use of big data and analytics requires skilled professionals who understand both the technical and strategic aspects of these tools. Organizations need to invest in training and development to build these capabilities.

Cybersecurity Technologies

In today's interconnected world, cybersecurity has become a critical concern for organizations of all sizes. As cyber threats grow more sophisticated, advanced cybersecurity tools and strategies are essential to protect sensitive information and maintain operational integrity. Let's break down the key components of cybersecurity technologies and illustrate how they are applied globally.

Core Components of Cybersecurity Technologies

Firewalls:

Firewalls act as a barrier between a trusted internal network and untrusted external networks, such as the internet. They monitor and control incoming and outgoing network traffic based on predetermined security rules. Imagine a corporate network as a castle. The firewall is the moat and walls that protect the castle from invaders. Only trusted entities (like approved data packets) are allowed to cross the moat.

Intrusion Detection Systems (IDS):

IDS monitor network traffic for suspicious activities and potential threats. They alert administrators when unusual patterns are detected, allowing for timely intervention. Think of IDS as security cameras within the castle. They don't just block invaders but continuously watch for any suspicious activity inside and outside the castle walls.

Endpoint Protection Platforms (EPP)

EPPs secure individual devices, such as laptops, smartphones, and tablets, by providing comprehensive protection against malware, ransomware, and other threats. They often include antivirus, anti-malware, and firewall functionalities. If each employee's laptop is a doorway into the castle, EPPs are like personal guards stationed at each door, ensuring only authorized and safe activities occur.

To understand how these technologies work in practice, let's look at Microsoft, a global technology giant renowned for its robust cybersecurity measures.

AI-Driven Threat Detection

Implementation: Microsoft employs artificial intelligence (AI) and machine learning to continuously monitor and analyze network traffic and user behavior. The AI models are trained to recognize patterns that indicate potential threats. If Microsoft's

AI detects an unusual login attempt from an unrecognized location or a sudden spike in data transfers, it flags these activities for review. This proactive approach helps in identifying threats before they can cause significant harm.

Regular Security Audits

During a security audit, Microsoft might discover that certain systems need updates or that new vulnerabilities have emerged. By addressing these issues promptly, Microsoft ensures its defenses remain strong against evolving threats.

Employee Training

Recognizing that human error is a common factor in security breaches, Microsoft invests heavily in employee training. This includes regular workshops, simulations, and updates on the latest cybersecurity practices. Employees learn how to identify phishing emails, use strong passwords, and follow best practices for data security. This reduces the risk of accidental breaches and ensures that all staff members contribute to maintaining a secure environment.

Global Application of Cybersecurity Technologies

While the example of Microsoft provides a detailed look at one organization's approach, these cybersecurity technologies are used globally across various sectors:

Banks and financial institutions use advanced firewalls, IDS, and EPP to protect customer data and financial transactions. Given the high stakes, these organizations often lead in adopting cutting-edge cybersecurity measures.

Example: A bank in Singapore might use real-time transaction monitoring powered by AI to detect and prevent fraud, ensuring the safety of its clients' assets.

Hospitals and healthcare providers must secure patient records and sensitive health data. Cybersecurity tools help prevent unauthorized access and ensure compliance with regulations such as the Health Insurance Portability and Accountability Act (HIPAA) in the United States.

Example: A hospital in Germany might use EPP to secure medical devices and patient data, while IDS monitors for any unusual access patterns that could indicate a breach.

Retailers handle large volumes of customer data, including payment information. Cybersecurity technologies protect this data from breaches and help maintain customer trust.

Example: An e-commerce platform in Brazil might use firewalls and EPP to secure its online storefront and customer databases, ensuring safe and seamless transactions.

Enhanced Regulatory Requirements

With the increasing complexity of global operations, regulatory requirements are becoming more stringent. Organizations must stay informed about evolving regulations and ensure compliance to avoid penalties and reputational damage.

Stricter Compliance Standards: Regulatory bodies are imposing more rigorous standards to protect consumers and ensure fair practices. Organizations must implement robust compliance programs to meet these standards. This involves conducting regular audits, maintaining accurate records, and providing training to employees on regulatory requirements.

A pharmaceutical company operating in multiple countries faces diverse regulatory requirements. To ensure compliance, the company implements a centralized compliance management system that tracks regulatory changes, schedules audits, and provides training modules for employees. This proactive approach helps the company avoid legal issues and maintain its market reputation.

Data Privacy Regulations: With the increasing focus on data privacy, organizations must comply with regulations such as the General Data Protection Regulation (GDPR) and the California Consumer Privacy Act (CCPA). This involves safeguarding personal data, obtaining consent for data collection, and providing individuals with the right to access and delete their data.

A social media platform updates its privacy policies and implements stringent data protection measures to comply with GDPR. This includes encryption of user data, regular security assessments, and transparent communication with users about how their data is used. By prioritizing data privacy, the platform builds trust with its users and avoids hefty fines.

Focus on Resilience

Building resilience is essential for organizations to withstand various risks and uncertainties. This involves developing robust risk management frameworks, fostering a risk-aware culture, and continuously improving practices.

Robust Risk Management Frameworks: Organizations need comprehensive frameworks that encompass all aspects of risk management, from identification to mitigation and monitoring. These frameworks should be flexible and adaptable to evolving risks.

A global manufacturing firm implements an enterprise risk management (ERM) framework that integrates risk management into all business processes. The framework includes regular risk assessments, scenario planning, and cross-functional risk committees. This holistic approach enables the firm to identify and address risks proactively.

Fostering a Risk-Aware Culture: Cultivating a culture that prioritizes risk management is crucial. This involves leadership commitment, employee engagement, and open communication. When everyone in the organization understands the importance of risk management, it becomes a collective responsibility.

A tech startup promotes a risk-aware culture by conducting regular training sessions, encouraging employees to report risks, and recognizing proactive risk management efforts. Leadership leads by example, demonstrating a commitment to risk management in decision-making processes. This culture empowers employees to take ownership of risk management and contribute to the company's resilience.

Continuous Improvement: Risk management is an ongoing process. Organizations must regularly review and update their risk management practices based on feedback and lessons learned. This involves conducting post-incident reviews, staying informed about emerging risks, and investing in new technologies.

A logistics company continuously improves its risk management practices by analyzing past incidents and implementing lessons learned. After experiencing a major supply chain disruption, the company reviews its response and identifies areas for improvement. It then updates its contingency plans, invests in advanced tracking technologies, and establishes stronger partnerships with suppliers. This iterative approach ensures the company is better prepared for future disruptions.

CONCLUSION

In summary, adapting to future uncertainties requires a proactive and dynamic approach to risk management. By leveraging advanced technologies like AI and data analytics, staying ahead of regulatory requirements, and building a resilient organizational culture, companies can navigate the complexities of a hybrid work environment and thrive in an ever-changing landscape. As the future unfolds, organizations that embrace innovation and continuous improvement will be best positioned to manage risks and seize opportunities.

AI and Machine Learning are revolutionizing risk management by providing powerful tools for data analysis, pattern recognition, and predictive modeling. Companies like Amazon demonstrate the practical applications of these technologies, showing how they can be used to manage complex global supply chains proactively. As these technologies continue to evolve, their impact on risk management will only grow, helping businesses navigate an increasingly uncertain world with greater confidence and resilience.

Cybersecurity technologies are crucial in safeguarding sensitive data and maintaining the integrity of operations in a digital world. By employing tools like firewalls, IDS, and EPP, organizations can protect themselves against a wide range of cyber threats. Real-world examples, such as Microsoft's comprehensive cybersecurity framework, demonstrate how these technologies are implemented to detect, prevent, and respond to security incidents effectively.

Whether in financial services, healthcare, retail, or any other sector, the principles of cybersecurity remain the same: proactive detection, robust defense mechanisms, and continuous improvement. As cyber threats evolve, so too must the technologies and strategies that protect against them, ensuring that organizations worldwide remain secure and resilient.

To conclude, adapting to future uncertainties requires a proactive and dynamic approach to risk management. By leveraging advanced technologies like AI and data analytics, staying ahead of regulatory requirements, and building a resilient organizational culture, companies can navigate the complexities of a hybrid work environment and thrive in an ever-changing landscape. As the future unfolds, organizations that embrace innovation and continuous improvement will be best positioned to manage risks and seize opportunities.

Chapter 10

CULTIVATING A RISK-READY CULTURE

As we conclude this comprehensive guide on risk management, it's clear that navigating the complexities of today's dynamic environment requires a proactive, well-rounded approach. From understanding the fundamentals to leveraging advanced technologies, effective risk management is essential for organizational resilience and long-term success.

Throughout this book, we've explored various facets of risk management, each contributing to a holistic strategy that organizations can adopt and adapt. Let's recap and reflect on the key insights from each chapter:

Chapter 1: Mapping the Risk Landscape

We began by laying the foundation, discussing the core principles of risk management: identification, assessment, mitigation, and monitoring. These steps form the bedrock of any risk management strategy, enabling organizations to systematically address potential threats. Real-world examples highlighted how organizations navigate the uncertainties of a hybrid work environment, underscoring the importance of flexibility and adaptability.

Chapter 2: Identifying the Unknowns

We delved into the diverse responsibilities of a risk manager in a hybrid work setting. Monitoring risks, communicating with stakeholders, implementing mitigation strategies, and conducting training sessions are critical tasks. The chapter emphasized the importance of maintaining effective communication across dispersed teams and leveraging agile methodologies to respond swiftly to emerging challenges.

Chapter 3: Assess, Mitigate, Monitor

We explored several risk management frameworks, including ISO 31000, COSO ERM, and agile risk management. Each framework offers unique strengths and applications, helping organizations tailor their risk management practices to specific needs. Brief case studies from the financial and technology sectors demonstrated how these frameworks are implemented in real-world scenarios, highlighting their practical value.

Chapter 4: Navigating Daily Challenges

Effective communication with global stakeholders is vital for maintaining engagement and alignment. This chapter provided strategies for managing stakeholders across different time zones and cultures, emphasizing the need for regular updates, cultural sensitivity, collaborative tools, and feedback mechanisms. Examples illustrated how organizations can build trust and foster a collaborative approach to risk management.

Chapter 5: Stakeholder Symbiosis

We examined detailed case studies from the financial and technology sectors, showcasing how organizations identified and mitigated risks using various frameworks and strategies. These real-world examples provided a deeper understanding of the practical application of risk management principles, highlighting successes and lessons learned.

Chapter 6: Framework Foundations

Handling real-time crises is a critical aspect of risk management. This chapter illustrated the steps involved in responding to a sudden data breach, from activating the incident response plan to conducting a post-incident review. Real-life examples from companies demonstrated the importance of swift action, effective communication, and continuous improvement in mitigating the impact of crises.

Chapter 7: Learning from the Past

We explored the role of technology in enhancing risk management practices. AI, machine learning, data analytics, collaboration platforms, and cybersecurity tools were discussed in detail, highlighting how these technologies can help organizations identify, assess, and mitigate risks more effectively. Examples from global companies demonstrated the practical benefits of integrating advanced technologies into risk management strategies.

Chapter 8: Crisis Command

Creating a culture that prioritizes risk management is crucial for long-term success. This chapter emphasized the importance of training programs, leadership commitment, open communication, and continuous improvement. Case studies from various industries illustrated how organizations foster a risk-aware culture, enabling them to proactively manage risks and enhance their resilience.

Chapter 9: Tech-Enabled Risk Mastery

The final chapter looked ahead, discussing future trends in risk management. Increased reliance on technology, enhanced regulatory requirements, and a focus on building resilient organizations were identified as key trends. We explored how organizations can stay ahead of these trends by adopting proactive, flexible, and forward-thinking risk management practices.

Chapter 10: Cultivating a Risk-Ready Culture

As we face an increasingly complex and uncertain world, the importance of robust risk management cannot be overstated. Organizations must be proactive, leveraging advanced technologies, adopting effective frameworks, and fostering a culture of continuous learning and improvement. By doing so, they can navigate uncertainties, mitigate risks, and seize opportunities for growth and success.

In closing, remember that risk management is not a one-time effort but an ongoing journey. It requires vigilance, adaptability, and a commitment to excellence. Whether you're a seasoned risk manager or new to the field, the principles and practices outlined in this book provide a roadmap for building resilient, forward-thinking organizations capable of thriving in the face of uncertainty. Embrace these strategies, stay informed about emerging trends, and continue to evolve your risk management practices. The future is uncertain, but with a proactive approach, you can navigate it with confidence and resilience

APPENDICES

Appendix A: Glossary of Risk Management Terms

Risk Identification: The process of finding, recognizing, and describing risks that could affect the achievement of an organization's objectives.

Risk Assessment: The overall process of risk identification, risk analysis, and risk evaluation.

Agile Risk Management: A dynamic approach to risk management that emphasizes flexibility, continuous improvement, and proactive responses.

Hybrid Work Environment: A flexible working arrangement where employees work both remotely and in-office.

Appendix B: Risk Management Frameworks

ISO 31000: Provides principles and guidelines for risk management applicable to any organization.

COSO ERM: A widely-used framework that defines essential components, suggests a common language, and provides clear direction and guidance for enterprise risk management.

NIST Cybersecurity Framework: A policy framework of computer security guidance for how private sector organizations in the US can assess and improve their ability to prevent, detect, and respond to cyber attacks.

Appendix C: Tools and Technologies

AI and Machine Learning: Tools for predictive analytics and proactive risk assessment, such as IBM Watson and TensorFlow.

Data Analytics Platforms: Tools like Power BI, Tableau, and Splunk for identifying patterns and trends in risk data.

Collaboration Tools: Platforms such as Slack, Microsoft Teams, and Asana that enhance communication and coordination in hybrid work environments.

Cybersecurity Tools: Solutions like Norton, McAfee, and Palo Alto Networks for advanced threat detection and incident response.

Appendix D: Case Study Summaries

Global Bank Corp.: Cybersecurity enhancements during a transition to hybrid work.

Tech Innovators Inc.: Supply chain risk management during the pandemic.

Software Solutions Ltd.: Agile risk management framework implementation.

Global Energy Corp.: ISO 31000 application in operational risk management.

HealthTech Innovations: Cybersecurity resilience building using the NIST framework.

Appendix E: Templates and Checklists

Risk Management Plan Template: A structured format to document identified risks, assessments, and mitigation plans.

Incident Response Plan Template: A detailed guide to handle incidents effectively, including roles, responsibilities, and steps.

Risk Assessment Checklist: A tool to ensure comprehensive risk evaluation, covering identification, analysis, and prioritization.

Appendix F: Training Programs

Sample Training Module: An outline of a training session on risk management basics.

Advanced Training Sessions: Detailed programs for training on specific frameworks like ISO 31000 and COSO ERM.

Cybersecurity Awareness Training: Modules for educating employees on best practices to prevent cyber threats.

Appendix G: Regulatory and Compliance Resources

GDPR Overview: Key points and compliance requirements for data protection in the EU.

HIPAA Summary: Essential information on health information privacy and security regulations in the US.

SOX Compliance: Guidelines for financial reporting and auditing standards in the US.

Appendix H: Further Reading and Resources

Books: "Enterprise Risk Management" by James Lam, "The Failure of Risk Management" by Douglas Hubbard.

Articles and Papers: Industry reports from Deloitte, PwC, and McKinsey on risk management trends.

Online Courses: Listings from Coursera, edX, and Udemy on risk management and cybersecurity.

Appendix I: Professional Associations

RIMS (Risk and Insurance Management Society): Membership benefits, contact information, and resources.

IRM (Institute of Risk Management): Overview of certifications, professional development programs, and contact details.

ISACA: Information on certifications like CISM (Certified Information Security Manager) and CRISC (Certified in Risk and Information Systems Control).

Appendix J: Frequently Asked Questions (FAQ)

What is Risk Management?: A primer on the basics of risk management and its importance.

How do Agile Frameworks Help in Risk Management?: Explanation of the benefits of agile methodologies in managing risks.

What are Common Cybersecurity Threats?: A list of typical cybersecurity risks and how to mitigate them.

ABOUT THE AUTHOR

Sanjay Thiyagarajan is a passionate advocate for risk management with a wealth of experience spanning diverse industries and global environments. With a career that has taken him from bustling financial districts in London to vibrant markets in Mumbai, Sanjay brings a unique perspective shaped by his extensive international exposure.

Throughout his career, Sanjay has held pivotal roles in risk management, leveraging his expertise to navigate complexities in sectors ranging from finance and technology to manufacturing and healthcare. His insights into global risk landscapes have been honed through practical experience in developing and implementing robust risk management strategies that mitigate uncertainties and enhance organizational resilience.

Sanjay's dedication to the field is evident not only in his professional endeavors but also in his commitment to sharing knowledge. As a thought leader, he regularly contributes to industry forums and publications, advocating for proactive risk management practices that align with evolving business landscapes.

A firm believer in continuous learning, Sanjay holds advanced degrees in Risk Management and Business Administration, complementing his hands-on experience with a solid academic foundation. His upcoming book promises to distill years of practical wisdom and strategic acumen into actionable insights, empowering readers to navigate the dynamic world of risk with confidence.

www.ingramcontent.com/pod-product-compliance
Lightning Source LLC
Chambersburg PA
CBHW052204220526
45471CB00004B/1811